HOW TO LISTEN
TO YOUR CAT

*The Complete Guide
to Communicating with
Your Feline Friend*

Kim O. Morgan

HOW TO LISTEN TO YOUR CAT: THE COMPLETE GUIDE TO COMMUNICATING WITH YOUR FELINE FRIEND

Library of Congress Cataloging-in-Publication Data

Morgan, K.O., 1957-
  How to listen to your cat : the complete guide to communicating with your feline friend / by K.O. Morgan.
      pages cm
Includes bibliographical references and index.
ISBN 978-1-60138-597-0 (alk. paper)
ISBN 1-60138-597-8 (alk. paper)
1. Cats--Behavior. 2. Human-animal communication. I. Title.
SF446.5.M64 2015
636.8--dc23
                        2015034262

Printed in the United States

PROJECT MANAGER: Melissa Shortman
ASSISTANT EDITOR: Melissa Shortman
INTERIOR LAYOUT: Antoinette D'Amore • addesign@videotron.ca
COVER DESIGN: Jackie Miller • sullmill@charter.net

Printed on Recycled Paper

Reduce. Reuse.
RECYCLE.

A decade ago, Atlantic Publishing signed the Green Press Initiative. These guidelines promote environmentally friendly practices, such as using recycled stock and vegetable-based inks, avoiding waste, choosing energy-efficient resources, and promoting a no-pulping policy. We now use 100-percent recycled stock on all our books. The results: in one year, switching to post-consumer recycled stock saved 24 mature trees, 5,000 gallons of water, the equivalent of the total energy used for one home in a year, and the equivalent of the greenhouse gases from one car driven for a year.

Over the years, we have adopted a number of dogs from rescues and shelters. First there was Bear and after he passed, Ginger and Scout. Now, we have Kira, another rescue. They have brought immense joy and love not just into our lives, but into the lives of all who met them.

We want you to know a portion of the profits of this book will be donated in Bear, Ginger and Scout's memory to local animal shelters, parks, conservation organizations, and other individuals and nonprofit organizations in need of assistance.

– Douglas & Sherri Brown,
President & Vice-President of Atlantic Publishing

Dedication

"When a man loves cats, I am his friend and comrade,
without further introduction."
~ Mark Twain

This book is dedicated to:

My mother, Shirley Nagele Morgan,
who got us our first cat, Tibby.

And to all the cats I've known and loved:

Tybalt, Sid Vicious, Sweet Pea, Golden, Lil Bit,
Hattie, Snickers, Charlie and Tomaki.

Table of Contents

Introduction **11**

Chatty Catty 12

Overview of This Book 13

**Chapter 1: Out of the Wild and Into the House
—How the Cat Became Our Pet** **17**

The Stealth Opportunist 20

Digging Into the Past to Understand
What Makes Today's Cat Tick...............................23

Making the leap into our lives 26

**Chapter 2: Myths, Misconceptions and Mysteries
About Cats and Owning Cats** **35**

Misconception: Cats Are a Low Maintenance Pet..........................36

Myth: Declawing is a Necessary But Minor Surgery 38

Myth: A Cat is a Free Spirit
Who Must be Free to Come and Go...............................41

Misconception: Cats Can Be Vegetarians............................43

Myth: Female Cats Should Have One Litter Before They
are Spayed, and Male Cats do Not Need to be Neutered 46

Myth: Cats are a Danger to Pregnant Women 51

Myth: Cats are a Danger to Babies
and Should Never be Around Them 53

Misconception: Cats Should be Free
to Come and Go 55

Myth: Cats Always Land on Their Feet 61

Myth: Cats and Dogs Don't Get Along 63

Misconception: Cats Are Not
as Affectionate as Dogs..66

Silly Superstitions That Persist to This Day....................................69

Whiskers give a cat balance 69

Cats have nine lives 71

Cats are nocturnal 72

Cats hate water 74

Black cats are unlucky 75

Cats are mean, sneaky and untrustworthy.....................................76

**Chapter 3: Choosing the Right Cat – and
What to do When a Cat Chooses You............ 81**

Kitten Cuteness or Cat Calmness...82

Domestic or Moggie Versus
Purebred or Pedigreed...87

Choosing a Breed..90

The mixed bag of mixed breeds 92

Feral cats: living life on the wild side 94

The Long and Short of It..98

The Silent Type Versus Chatty Catty 99

Loner Versus Lover..100

Adopting the Special Needs Cat 103

Choosing Your Healthy Cat and What to Look For.....................106

Sometimes the Cat Picks You 108

**Chapter 4: Meow is Just One Word –
Understanding What Your Cat
is Saying From Head to Tail.......................... 111**

The Cat's Meow 113

Body Posturing: Speaking and Understanding
Your Cat's First Language 115

Tummy rollover *116*

Cat rub *116*

Needing to knead you *117*

The tale of the tail *118*

Head to head *120*

The Eyes Are a Mirror to a Cat's Soul 121

Getting an Earful 123

Watch the Whiskers 124

Cat Smiles and Kitty Lips..126

Licking Means Love 127

Kitty Presents 130

Chapter 5: Teaching Your Cat to Speak Human............ 133

Name Calling, Verbal Commands,
and Word Associations..135

Clickety Click 139

Cat Sign Language 143

Communicating Through Grooming and Petting....................146

Play Ball 148

Tricking your cat *151*

Learning to Speak Meow...155

Chapter 6: What Your Cat Doesn't Say
Could Harm It 159

Outside the Box...159

Constipation..*161*

Urinary Tract Infection *163*

Renal Failure...*164*

Cystitis..*166*

Urinary Tract Stones...*167*

Declawing *168*

Down in the Dumps..168

Common Cat Diseases 171

Hyperthyroid disease 171

Cancer 172

Diabetes..173

Feline Leukemia 174

Heart disease..174

Parasites..175

Upper respiratory infection 177

Feline Aids 178

Feline infectious peritonitis 179

Feline distemper...180

Typical Warning Signs of Sickness 181

Lethargy 182

Repetitive vomiting or gagging 182

Stops eating...183

Diarrhea 183

Blood in the urine 183

Sudden weight loss or weight gain 183

Drinking more water and urinating more frequently 184

Gum changes 184

Runny eyes or nose..184

Shortness of breath, panting or coughing............................184

Stiffness when moving...185

Ear itching 185

Fever...186

Lumps or abnormal growths...186

Disorientation 186

Back leg dragging or paralysis...187

Matty coat or skin changes..187

Play it safe...187

Chapter 7: Teaching Your Cat
the Rules of the House 189

Learning to Learn 190

Make the lesson fun *191*

Feeding on Your Time – Not Your Cat's.............................194

Don't Discipline – Discourage 198

Drawing the Line Between Play and Aggression....................201

A bored cat is an unhappy cat *203*

**Chapter 8: Funny Antics – Why Cats Can Be
Amusing, Hilarious, Endearing ...
and Infuriating!... 205**

Sleep Gymnastics..205

Blocking out the world...*207*

Bare belly *207*

Cuddle buddies..*208*

Zonking out on your clothes or shoes *208*

Sitting Like a Thanksgiving Turkey and
Other Funny Cat Positions...209

Boxes, Bags and Other Non Cat Toys...................................210

Alarm Clock Cats...212

Toilet Paper Cats...216

The Kitty Art of Opening Doors..219

The Need to be Near Us 220

Kneading us *221*

**Chapter 9: Going Along For the Ride –
Talking Down Your Anxious Cat 223**

Keep Your Cat Contained 223

Ready, Set, Go 226

Cats on the Move..227

**Chapter 10: First Impressions –
How to Introduce Your Cat
to a New Member of the Family............... 233**

Baby on Board...234

Changing Family Dynamics 237

Adding a New Pet to the Fold..239

Creating a Clowder 239

Adding a dog to the mix 243

Chapter 11: There's a Tiger in Every Cat 247

Taming the Wild Side 250

Testing the territorial boundaries 251

How fixing can fix aggression –
and save lives at the same time 253

Sitting on a Different Branch in the Evolutionary Tree 254

Chapter 12: Keeping Your Kitty Safe 257

Keep Your Cat Indoors – No Matter What It Tells You 257

Curiosity Can Kill Your Cat:
Beware of Household Hazards 260

The Dangerous Holidays 263

The Dreaded But Necessary Vet Visit 265

The vaccine controversy 266

Chapter 13: When it is Time to Say Goodbye 269

Making Life Easier for Your Senior Cat 270

Being There When Your Cat Needs You Most 272

A new kid on the block 273

Conclusion 275

Glossary 277

Author Biography 283

Index 285

Introduction

Humans, it is believed, actively domesticated dogs and horses. We went out, caught them, and tamed them in order to benefit from what they could do for us. In return, we provided them with food and care and later affection, but the domestication of dogs and horses, as well as farm animals, was one that had to be planned and put into action, and involved breaking the wild spirit, training, and breeding out the wild over time.

But the cat, true to its independent nature, domesticated itself. It sought out humans as a means of survival, and injected itself into human lives. We didn't seek the cat; the cat sought us. In other words, the cat invited itself in rather than the other way around.

Scientists trace the domestication of cats to about 12,000 years ago when humans became farmers, and opportunistic mice, rats and other small creatures came on the scene to eat the crops that people so carefully cultivated and stored. Cats, ever the resourceful survivor and opportunist, quickly figured out that where people live, so do rodents, which were until modern times the feline's main food source. As a result, humans and cats formed a mutually beneficial bond where each provided the other with what was needed — pest control in exchange for a never ending food source.

This bond evolved into fondness, a trait that modern cats seem to thrive on. In the process, cats have become the most popular pet in the world; found in homes the world over, with an estimation of over 600,000 cats living on six continents.

Chatty Catty

Some cats are more vocal than others. For example, the Siamese breed is known for being very talkative, bordering on loud. But whether you own a chatty catty or a quieter feline, communicating with your cat is vital. Developing a language with your cat can help it to adjust to your home life, can enrich your relationship, and can deepen the bond between you.

Cats are highly intelligent and able to learn hand signals, words, and even facial expressions. In the process, owners often learn their particular cat's language, body cues and even what different sounds mean. This mutual communication helps to strengthen the bond between you, make your cat a better pet, and make the experience of a human-cat relationship more pleasurable.

Communicating with a cat is a complex undertaking, but one that will evolve naturally provided that you are open to learning the language of cats. In fact, it is not unusual for cat owners to talk to their cats and understand what their cats are saying when the cat talks back. This human-cat conversation is a mutual exchange: while you are learning to speak cat, your cat is learning to speak human by picking up your cues, expressions, words, body language and signals.

Not only will this make the relationship with your cat more interesting and pleasurable, but learning to speak cat will improve the well being of your feline. Cats can tell us when they're happy, sad, excited, sick, hungry or bored — as long as we are listening and are in tune to what they are trying to tell us. Sometimes life or death clues can be apparent when we know what those clues are. And sometimes, our relationships with our cats depend entirely on whether or not we take the time to learn their language.

Overview of This Book

One of the keys in understanding our feline friends is understanding their history and how the whole human-cat relationship came about. This book will discuss in detail the historical steps that occurred in the domestication of cats and how the mutual communication between humans and cats evolved.

The reader will also learn some misconceptions about felines that were believed through history and that are often believed to this day. Those misunderstandings can interfere in the loving bond that can be experienced with a pet cat and even harm a feline in the process.

The book begins with listing the do's and do not's involved in being a cat owner, and what process should be followed when choosing a cat in order to make sure a potential cat owner picks the right breed (or mixed breed), personality, size, and other traits to ensure that the cat fits in with the owner's lifestyle and to prevent the tragic all too common occurrence of turning a feline over to an animal shelter where it may be euthanized.

The book discusses in detail the universal language of cats, including what certain sounds, body languages, nuances, bad and good behavior, and expressions mean. Cat communication, particularly communication through cat body language, is not always as obvious as that of dogs. This books hopes to uncover the often-mysterious ways in which cats talk to us, which can only benefit the cat-owner relationship in the long run. It also details how you can train your cat to communicate with you in other ways, which will deepen the special bond between you. Cat feelings are also detailed, including how to tell if your pet is depressed, unhappy, sick or stressed, and what to do if your cat is displaying these traits, some of which can be life threatening.

Although some people believe that cats cannot be trained, this is far from the case. Cat training is discussed in detail, as is learning how to introduce your cat to a new member of the family or a new home, in order to make the transition as stress-free and harmonious as possible.

How cats keep us entertained, healthy and happy, and what experts say about the language and the importance of communicating with your cat, are also covered. Case studies and interviews detailing this expertise can be found in the book. Finally, how to know when it's time to say goodbye to your ailing or elderly cat and what you can expect to experience during this sad process, are also discussed.

Out of the Wild and Into the House —How the Cat Became Our Pet

I t was once believed that cats became domesticated around the time of the Egyptians, about 4,000 years ago. And while there is no doubt that the cat had a favored position in Egyptian civilization, including often being worshipped or revered as gods and goddesses, being mummified along with their owners, and imposing the death penalty on anyone who killed a cat, the domestication of cats actually occurred earlier in history—about 12,000 years ago.

The mystery surrounding the evolution of cats from wild to domestic is largely due to the lack of evidence for when and how this took place. This is because humans have rarely eaten cats, so little substantiated proof exists in the form of bones found in human diets. In addition, there is little difference in the skeletal remains of wild cats and domestic cats, which makes determining which skeleton is a wild cat and which is a housecat difficult.

Archeologists changed their beliefs that cats had an earlier history than originally thought around 1983 when an 8,000-year-old cat jawbone was discovered on the Island of Cypress. Because cats do not take naturally to water, this led archeologists to believe that domestication probably occurred even earlier than 8,000 years ago. Then a discovery was made in 2004, again in Cyprus, at another site that aged the domestication of cats to about 9,500 years ago.

Today, scientists believe that today's domestic cat originated in the Fertile Crescent, or Middle East, and spread to Asia, and is a descendent of a wildcat called *Felis sylvestris,* which translated means, "cat of the woods." It is believed that the cat came out of the wild about 12,000 years ago and grew out of a mutually beneficial relationship between humans and cats that was based on agriculture.

While humans were involved in both the domestication of dogs and cats (as well as other animals), this process occurred for dif-

ferent reasons. Humans actively domesticated the dog's ancestor, the wolf, when man was a hunter-gatherer. Humans went
out and sought the company of wolves and over time, tamed the
dog's ancestor. These early dog/ wolves helped with the hunt in
tracking and attacking other animals that humans ate. Dogs also
protected the camps of humans in exchange for free food. Over
time and several generations, this wolf descendant was tamed or
became used to living with or near humans, and in the centuries
that followed, humans mastered breeding certain wolf and dog
traits in or out.

This domestication of the wolf was a deliberate act on the part
of humans, as was the domestication of horses, cattle, pigs and
other domestic animals. Mankind may have started with wolf
cubs that they attempted to tame and raise as companion animals
and protectors. But in the case of the cat, the domestication was
a matter of chance and it happened later in the game, when man
became a farmer and domesticated crops.

Once humans understood how plants reproduced and how they
could be cultivated and grown as a food source, they began to
settle in one place. Settlements, towns and cities sprung up and
along with these communities came the need to store surplus
crops for future eating. This attracted mice, rats and other rodents. It also attracted wild cats whose diet was mainly made
up of small animals. Humans at some point realized that if they
allowed the cats to hang around, they had a pest control resource
that did not require being fed the grain that it was protecting.
Thus began the relationship between humans and cats. It could
be said that humans did not domesticate cats, but rather, cats domesticated themselves.

Of course, not all cats joined in the fray. But those who displayed
friendlier, calmer, docile traits were favored by humans over cats

that were more wild and aggressive and less sociable. Over time, humans learned to breed certain traits in or out, and cats came to view humans with affection since, as is the case with all domestic animals, food means love.

Today, the cat is number one in popularity, owning one third of households in the United States alone. This affection of cats is shared the world over; it is believed that 600 million felines worldwide are kept as pets. And while scientists have an idea of when this domestication occurred, the exact process still remains as mysterious as the cat itself.

The Stealth Opportunist

Most cat owners would agree that you don't pick a cat – the cat picks you. Unlike dogs, who easily show affection to anyone who is willing to pet, brush, walk and feed them, cats can be picky about who they give their love to. True to their intelligent nature, it was the cat who injected itself into human lives and not the other way around. Luckily for those of us today who enjoy the company of cats, humans thousands of years ago were astute enough to see the advantage of having a built-in pest controller hanging around.

But the evolution of housecats actually occurred long before humans came on the scene. It is believed that wild and domesticated cats share a common prehistoric ancestor, a medium sized cat-like animal (although not specifically a cat as we know it) called *Pseudaelurus*, which evolved in Central Asia and lived about 11 million years ago. Low sea levels allowed this creature to migrate into Africa, and North America where it made its way down to South America, and also into Europe. During this time, some two to three million years ago, the evolutionary tree of this cat-like animal developed into three separate branches: saber-toothed cats that would become today's big cat, including lions, tigers and jaguars; conical toothed cats that would evolve into medium-sized cats, including the leopard, cougar, and puma; and the smaller basal toothed cat whose ancestor was the wildcat *Felis sylvestris* mentioned earlier and whose descendants are today's housecat.

How and why these three evolutionary branches occurred is a mystery but more than likely it has to do with habitat, diet and climate, which are the basis for evolutionary changes in most animals. The difficulty in solving the cat's exact evolutionary process is linked to the fact that there is very little physiological difference between wild cats and domestic cats – their inherited traits are more similar than not.

Amazingly, out of the many various times of cats that evolved over millions of years, only one would become domesticated. However, other than a housecat's willingness and desire to live among humans, you only have to watch a wild feline today to see that the tiger, lion, jaguar, cheetah, leopard, cougar and other wild cats share many of the same traits and habits that our pet cats display. Most purr, all are self bathing, most have retractable claws, all sleep the majority of their day away, all go through the motions of marking their territories, and all enjoy the play involved in the hunt. In fact, today's domestic cat's ability to survive makes it almost identical to its wild cousins and not unlike its wild ancestors.

Similar, however, does not mean the same. Domesticated felines have adapted to live among humans, whereas wild cats have not. This adaptation was a matter of survival, starting with humans appreciating the necessary pest control offered by cats and cats, in turn, appreciating the free food. Along the way, a bond was created based on mutual affection, and in the 20th century, with the advent of other means of controlling rodents, the cat became our pet and nothing more. Today, most cat owners are horrified when their felines bring them presents of rodents. And most cat owners and veterinarians agree that allowing our cats to hunt and eat mice, rats, birds and other small animals is not healthy and can cause serious illnesses.

Even so, cats have adapted to being human pets while still displaying wild tendencies. Perhaps that is what makes them so fascinating to us and may be one reason why they have become the most popular pet. Like their wild counterparts, cats hunt, pounce, and can be territorial. They are partially nocturnal and they love to play. And most cat owners have experienced an occasional scratch or bite from their feline friends.

Ironically, other than affection and companionship, cats offer no helpful or needed service to humans. For example, dogs became domesticated because they offered us protection and assistance with hunting, and many still do. Cows, sheep, chickens and goats became domesticated because they gave us milk, clothing and meat, which they continue to do. Horses offered us transportation and labor, and while many horses today are used solely for the pleasure of riding, many others today continue to provide us with assistance or use. But cats do none of these services or benefits. Instead, cats injected themselves into our lives thousands of years ago simply because rodents feeding on our grain stores provided them with a ready-made meal and they in turn gave us rodent control. But today, our felines provide no other service except companionship and love.

Once humans stopped needing cats for pest control, our attraction to them may have simply been based on characteristics that many humans find endearing and appealing, traits that we still are drawn to. For one thing, their small size makes them easy to keep, especially today when space is a premium in our ever crowded world. Cats also have features that humans find cute and/or childlike. They have small faces and bodies with wide round eyes, and expressive ears. They rub against us when they are happy and purr when they are content, qualities that humans interpret as loving. Most cats are very social and need the human touch, which many humans find hard to resist. Felines do not require much food, and they do not need to be walked for exercise and to go to the bathroom outside. Their natural ability to use a litter box makes their eliminations less work. In a nutshell, cats are easy, which is ideal for many people who do not have the time to spend on the higher maintenance dog.

Digging Into the Past to Understand What Makes Today's Cat Tick

The belief that the Egyptians first domesticated felines around 3,500 years ago was eventually disproved via DNA testing.

When applied to today's cats versus their wild ancestors of the past, evidence from the molecular biology field puts feline ancestry between 8,000 and 15,000 years ago. Given that 15,000-20,000 years ago is when modern humans probably arrived on the evolutionary scene, many scientists and archeologists believe that cats were probably domesticated closer to 8,000 to 10,000 years ago rather than 15,000 years ago, since humans were first hunter-gatherers and had no need to form a bond with cats prior to cultivating and storing crops, although this is up for debate. Therefore, 10,000 years ago is often the timeframe used when determining when cats came to live among us.

Many archeologists believe that cats were first tamed in the Middle East, specifically the Fertile Crescent, which covers Iraq through Jordan, Syria, Israel and down to Egypt. However, Cyprus has also been sighted as a location where the domestication of cats may have occurred, although some question this premise simply because Cyprus is a series of islands not connected to any mainland, and given the abhorrence of most felines for water, it leaves one to wonder how cats would have migrated to this island nation. It is also difficult to determine if the bone fragments found of cats from this time period of 8,000 years ago, are indeed housecats, rather than wild cats. If so, then they were probably transported to these islands as captives or pets of humans.

Scientists have hypothesized that the emergence of today's house mouse probably coincided with the domestication of wild cats. There are more than 30 species of mice worldwide, but only the house mouse evolved to exploit our readymade storage of available food and the warm, dry housing we provided when storing this grain. As we transported food to other parts of the world, house mice came along for the ride, and with them, the need for cats in order to keep their populations in check and protect our food supplies.

Cats are not the only ones who hunted mice and were attracted to the grain storage bins that housed them, however. Foxes, jackals, birds of prey and domesticated dogs were also predators of mice. But wild cats held the advantage over these other hunters in that these felines are nocturnal, as are mice, whereas dogs, jackals and most birds of prey (with the exception of the owl) are not. And while foxes are also nocturnal, cats see better in the dark. Add in the cat's agility and speed of attack, and they became the dominant and preferred rodent controller.

Even so, which species of wildcat *did* domesticated cats descend from? While it is agreed that all cats – large and small – share a common prehistoric ancestor, and that the housecat specifically descended from the basal toothed wildcat, *Felis sylvestris*, this would not account for the varied DNA found in today's many breeds of domesticated cats. This variation in DNA is, according to many scientists, the result of domesticated felines interbreeding with other wildcats since all species of cats are able to breed and reproduce with each other. Good examples today are the *Liger* and the *Tigon*. *Ligers* are the result of a male lion breeding with a female tiger, which if a male is the resulting offspring, it is usually sterile but a female offspring can reproduce; whereas a *Tigon* is the result of a male tiger mating with a female lion, and in this case a male *Tigon* offspring would be able to reproduce, but a female *Tigon* would not. It should be noted that lions and tigers rarely breed with each other in the wild since their habitats are almost always on separate continents, with the exception of a few places such as southern India where lions and tigers can both be found.

Making the leap into our lives

It has been difficult to pinpoint exactly when humans and cats developed mutual affection for each other. Certainly, Egyptians adored and even worshipped cats, often mummifying them when cats passed and enacting laws that promised punishment for deliberately killing a cat.

Perhaps the domestication of cats goes beyond pest control. In all parts of the world and throughout history, humans appear to have desired relationships with animals beyond what services they could provide. Even in remote areas of the Amazon today, many native peoples adopt wild baby animals and keep them as pets, a universal occurrence found the world over among cultures that have had no contact with each other.

Still, it is believed that Egyptian cats are the main ancestors of today's domesticated cats. This premise is likely because while Cyprus is viewed as the place where domestication or taming of wildcats may have first taken a stronghold, Egypt is the only place in the world where there is evidence on a large scale basis of deliberate relationships with cats. Whether those cats displayed more wild traits than today's cats is unknown. They certainly were larger than modern housecats, and their stripped coats made them indistinguishable from small wildcats of the area, except that they were affectionate and did not fear humans.

Keeping cats as pets, however, did not occur large scale outside of Egypt until about 2,500 years ago when Egypt first fell under Greek control, and then Roman rule, and the practice spread to the eastern and northern areas of the Mediterranean. There, cats likely bred with other wildcat or semi domesticated species in the area. This is not to say that other areas of the world did not domesticate cats or keep them as pets, especially since they were useful in keeping the rodent population in check. But it was the Egyptians who elevated the status of the housecat to something beyond just pest controllers.

Paintings of cats that appear as part of the household began appearing in Greece and the Roman Empire about 2,400 years ago, where felines also became associated with goddesses. As sea routes invoked increase trading, cats may have spread via ships to Indonesia, India, China and other parts of Asia, and into Europe. Interestingly, many Asian cats' DNA today reveals that they shared a common ancestor with European cats.

The Romans are often cited as the source for bringing cats across the English Channel and into Great Britain when they ruled the island nation from 43 to 409 A.D. But discoveries of cat and mouse bones from an earlier time dispute this theory. In Southern England, the bones from these hunters and hunted indicate that cats may have roamed England about 2,300 years ago, probably brought there from the Phoenicians of the Mediterranean, who briefly visited the British Isles.

Wherever cats roamed, they were valued for their rodent catching skills. The exception to this is during the Middle Ages, when the Roman Catholic Church decreed cats to be synonymous with pagan worship and heresy, probably due to the cat's connection to Egyptian times when it was worshipped as a deity. The 13th to 15th centuries proved to be a dark period for felines, one where cats, particularly black ones, witchcraft and Satan were closely associated and their survival in Europe was threatened. Millions of cats were tortured and killed, and in some areas of Europe, wiped out.

This view of demonizing cats was not shared universally, however. In Britain, cats continued to be appreciated for their pest controlling skills, and the Eastern Orthodox Church and Islam viewed felines with great affection, often writing and creating art about them. In fact, one of the earliest homeless shelters for cats was in Cairo, Egypt in 1280 A.D. Ironically, the black cat, the main bane of the Catholic Church, is common today in Europe, the Middle East and Africa.

It was during the Middle Ages that the cat went from being a larger domestic animal that retained some of its wildness to the smaller feline we know today. This may or may not be due to the persecution they suffered, but a 70 percent shrinkage in bone length appears to have occurred during this time, with no absolute reason why.

Cats were again persecuted in 17th century Great Britain, often being burned alive with full consent of the Catholic Church, again because of the perceived link to witchcraft, paganism and Satanism. But by the 18th century, cats began to grow in popularity, particularly in France and England, often winding up in the paintings of royalty. The affection for cats grew, with Queen Victoria keeping many cats in the late 19th century and Mark Twain in the U.S. often writing about how the cat was more honorable than man.

In any case, the evolution of the cat, from wild to domesticated, is a story of a clever opportunist: first as a pest controller, later as a companion and/or religious symbol, and finally as a domestic animal dependent on humans for affection and survival. This ability to evolve into a beloved pet is testament to the housecat's adaptability and its evolutionary success. Today, cats are the most popular pet in the world, thanks to their low maintenance care, their small size, and their adaptable personalities.

INTERVIEW WITH AN ANIMAL SHELTER WORKER:

Ann Graves began her career in the field of animal welfare as a volunteer for the Humane Society for Seattle/King County in 1991. Realizing she wanted to work with animals full time, she left her job at UPS and earned her Bachelor of Science degree in Zoology from the University of Washington in 1998. In 2000, she began working at the Seattle Animal Shelter and is currently the Manager of Field Services there. "After going back to school and getting my undergrad degree, I considered vet school but my heart was with shelter animals. I wanted a career where I could make a difference for many animals, although I had no idea what that career was or would look like. I was hired at Seattle Animal Shelter in 2000 as an Animal Care Officer where I worked in the shelter caring for the animals, getting strays back to owners, and adopting orphaned animals into new homes. In 2003, I became an animal control officer, now called humane animal law enforcement officers to more accurately reflect our role in the community. In 2004 I was promoted to Enforcement Supervisor and in 2013 became the Manager of Field Services, managing the enforcement unit here at SAS."

What is the most difficult part of your job?

The most difficult part of my job is seeing animals suffering from abuse and neglect on a regular basis. The best part of my job is being in a position to do something about it on a number of levels.

Why should people sterilize their cats?

Cats who are not sterilized can contribute to a multitude of nuisance issues, such as loudly vocalizing when in season, roaming, fighting, and reproducing which contributes to the huge number of kittens and cats entering local animal shelters every year. Males that fight each other for territory or females are more prone to life-threatening infections such as abscesses and diseases such as FIV. Females are more prone to the health risks that come with reproduction including difficulty or death while queening, breast tumors and pyometra, which is an infection in the uterus. Cats that roam are also at a greater risk of poisonings, whether accidental or intentional, as well as predation by wildlife or domestic dogs, and being hit by cars.

Cats that are sterilized are more likely to live longer, healthier lives because they are not prone to the activities that lead to such significant health risks. They are more likely to be kept as indoor pets, which is safer for them and less bothersome to neighbors who don't want someone else's cats lounging on the lawn furniture or defecating in their garden.

What are some of the persistent myths regarding sterilizing cats?

Primarily that their personality will change and they will get fat. While general personality doesn't change, the behavior driven by the urge to mate and reproduce is curtailed by sterilization. Like all animals, too many calories and not enough exercise is what contributes to obesity, not being spayed or neutered.

Sterilizing cats seems to be less of a priority for some in our society than sterilizing dogs. Cats are sometimes seen as an animal that normally just comes and goes at will and should be allowed to roam, which means that much of the unwanted activity that comes with being unsterilized occurs outside the view or knowledge of the owner.

How many cats are euthanized each year?

According to statistics from the American Society For The Prevention Of Cruelty To Animals (ASPCA), about 1.4 million cats are euthanized in animal shelters in the United States each year.

What are the benefits of adopting a cat from a shelter rather than a breeder?

When a person adopts a cat from a shelter, they are literally saving that life. Often cats are spayed and neutered prior to coming into the shelter or at the time of adoption, which can save the adopter money, depending on the policies of each shelter. Adopting from a shelter overall can be much less expensive than buying from a breeder. Some people may not feel prepared for an 18-year or longer commitment, so adopting an older cat can make sense. Adopting an adult cat can also provide relief from the antics (often nocturnal) of kittens and juvenile cats that cause considerable loss of sleep.

Is it important to neuter male cats as well as females? If so, why?

Yes, it is absolutely important to neuter male cats. Many people who have an unaltered male cat that is allowed to roam do not see the impact their one cat is having on an entire community. One female cat can only have one litter of kittens at a time and is reproductively unavailable from the time of impregnation through a period time post queening. But one male can impregnate multiple females during that same time, directly contributing to a much higher number of unplanned, unwanted kittens than a single female is capable of.

Unsterilized male cats will fight with sterilized male or female cats for territory, causing unnecessary injuries and spreading disease. Unaltered male cats are also likely to be more of a nuisance to neighbors through a multitude of behaviors and activities that are driven by their need to mate.

Should housecats be allowed to roam?

This is a topic that is often debated in communities grappling with issues ranging from increasing numbers of unowned feral cats, to shelters overburdened with incoming cats and kittens, to wildlife officials and enthusiasts concerned about the predation of native birds and other wildlife. Many would argue that it is natural for cats to roam and to confine them to being indoor-only is a cruel thing to do. And for some people free roaming cats help keep unwanted rodent populations from increasing.

One compromise that is gaining in popularity is the concept of cat enclosures which seems to give cats and communities the best of both worlds. Something as simple as an enclosure along the side of a house with a cat door giving access in and out of the house to an elaborate set up with a fully enclosed yard. This keeps the cats from engaging in nuisance behaviors in the neighborhood, keeps them safe from dangers inherent to roaming, and provides a combination of indoor and outdoor living.

Cats that are kept as indoor-only pets tend to live healthier, longer lives, and with toys and stimulation through playing with each other and their humans, window perches, and a growing array of activities, they adapt well to living within a household rather than roaming outside.

Do you think Humane Education should be a part of a shelter's adoption program and why?

Yes, Humane Education should be a part of all adoption processes. It can be as simple as an adoption questionnaire and application process which opens up a dialogue between shelter staff or volunteers and those who seek to adopt, to a full fledged Humane Education program that visits schools. The millions of orphaned animals in shelters around the United States rely on those of us who work and volunteer in animal shelters to provide Humane Education so that people understand that an animal is a commitment for a lifetime, not an urge to be filled and then forgotten. Part of that education also needs to be supportive of people who have the desire to keep their animals but are struggling to do so, either due to pet behavioral issues they need help dealing with or some unforeseen hardship.

Myths, Misconceptions and Mysteries About Cats and Owning Cats

he story of humans and cats began with agriculture, but has evolved into something quite different. In the beginning we used felines for their prowess in catching rodent threats to our food supplies and they used us as a free meal ticket. But today, the relationship between people and cats runs deep, with strong emotional ties. We don't need cats for our survival, but they have come to enrich our lives and we enjoy their company. They, on the other hand, have more or less lost their wild hunting abilities (although many a housecat allowed to go outside is adept at catching and killing birds and rodents, but this is usually for fun and not for survival), and have come to depend on humans for food, water and shelter, *and* for affection. Cats, it seems, want and need to have a relationship with the human species, and many humans want and need to have a relationship with them — so much so, that cats have become the most popular pet worldwide.

Still, many myths and misconceptions persist when it comes to owning a cat. And some humans are also uncomfortable with the cat's mysterious nature. But if your goal is to have a better relationship with your cat, that means improving the communications between you. The way to do that is to first dispel common myths and misconceptions that have pervaded and surrounded cats for centuries.

Misconception: Cats Are a Low Maintenance Pet

Probably one of the biggest misconceptions about cats is that they require little care outside of putting down a food bowl once or twice a day. While it is true that cats do not require the physical demands that dogs do, such as daily walks and bathroom breaks, felines still need emotional nourishment, brushing, attention, petting, toys to play with, and a clean litter box.

The misunderstanding that cats need little care may stem from their independent nature that fools some humans into thinking that cats need little beyond the bare minimum of food, water and shelter. The fact is cats are no different than people — some are more independent than others. Some like to cuddle and others do not. Some need constant attention, while others want attention when they want it and on their terms. Some are highly intelligent, some are average, and some are, well, not the sharpest claw in the room.

It is true that cats are more independent than say a dog, or a human child for that matter. They also can be left alone for longer periods of time than dogs since they do not need to be walked twice or three times a day in order to go to the bathroom. Their care is also less time consuming — they don't need baths on a weekly basis, for example. But easier care does not mean minimal care. Cats have a whole array of habits, needs and demands that must be met.

Take bathroom breaks, for instance. While it is true that cats do not need to be taken outside in order to eliminate, there is litter box etiquette that must be addressed in order to maintain a good relationship with your cat.

For one thing, placement of the litter box is very important since cats, like people, are self conscious about having an audience in the bathroom. Therefore, in deference to a cat's need for bathroom privacy, the litter box should be put in areas that are easy for your cat to get to, but away from human traffic. If it is not possible for a cat to have an entire area as its bathroom (such as a laundry room or mud room for example), then at least make sure that you place the litter box in the corner of the room or a part of the room that provides some privacy.

Also make sure—and this cannot be emphasized enough—that the litter box is nowhere near where your cat sleeps or eats. This is a huge no-no for cats since their smelling abilities are as tuned as any dog's, and to have the place they eliminate in smelling distance of where they bed or eat is tantamount to cat torture. This is why many cats in animal shelters often get depressed, which lowers their immune systems and can then lead to illness and even death. Usually the cat is housed in a tiny cage, along with its food and litter box, and for a cat, that is hell on earth.

Myth: Declawing is a Necessary But Minor Surgery

The declawing controversy has raged for decades, with one side arguing that without it, cats will claw up and destroy the furniture and it is the price a cat must pay in order to be adopted, and

the other side stating the declawing is unnatural, painful and dangerous and can result in lifelong trauma.

The truth is, declawing is major surgery and involves either surgically removing the first joint of each of a cat's toes or the latest technique, surgically lasering off where the nail attaches to the toe. In the past, many veterinarians presented this surgery as no big deal, a minor procedure that simply involves a few days of sore toes that require soft newspaper rather than litter in the litter box until the toes have healed.

Today, many veterinarians are more cautious about declawing, and even more either refuse to do the surgery or are willing to offer the cons to this surgery. Some cities and states have banned declawing, and many animal shelters make adopters sign an agreement promising to never declaw their adopted cat.

This is because all surgery involves risks. Declawing involves anesthesia, and whenever you put an animal or a person under, there is a possibility of death; the smaller the animal, the greater the risk. In addition, if declawing surgery is not done properly, nerves can be damaged in the toes and the cat will forever be in pain. Also, claws are a cat's defense mechanism, and cats that have been declawed tend to bite more and harder than cats that have their natural claws.

Cats do need to claw. It is a way to shorten their nails and since the paws are where some of a cat's scent glands are, clawing is a way to mark territory. Because of this, many declawing advocates claim that many cats won't use scratching posts, finding furniture and carpet much more appealing outlets to satisfy their need to scratch. But usually this is the fault of the owner not providing enough scratching posts and not placing the posts in the right area of the home.

The solution is really a commonsense one. If you have one or two scratching posts in one or two rooms but not in all of your rooms, and your cat happens to be in another room and feels the need to claw, it is not going to think, "Hmmm, the scratching post is in the living room so I'd better go there to do my scratching." Instead, your cat will scratch on whatever is readily available, and if that is the couch or curtains, so be it. But if you provide a scratching post in every room, on that is at least two feet tall and is made up of a material such as rope or of a nubby consistency that your cat can really get its claws into, your cat will tend to go for the scratching post instead. You can also reinforce using the post by rubbing it with catnip.

Another way to lessen your cat scratching up your furniture is to make sure you keep its nails trimmed. Cats scratch on posts and other things as a way of shortening overgrown nails. The trick can be getting your cat used to having its nails trimmed. If you adopt a cat as a kitten, then the task is a little easier. If your cat is an adult by the time you adopt it, then start out trimming the nails of one paw at a time and following the procedure up with a tasty treat. Eventually, your cat will associate nail trimming with something good to eat.

If you are still determined to declaw your cat, then make sure you only have the front paws done. Cats must have some defenses and they must have a means of scratching themselves, which is done by the back paws. This may sound like commonsense, but animal shelters do occasionally see cats come in with all four paws declawed. The idea that a vet would actually perform this surgery on the back paws is hard to fathom, but it does occur.

It should go without saying that if your cat is declawed, never let it go outside. You have just removed its main form of protection, and it could be helpless if attacked by another cat or a dog. If you adopt a cat that is already declawed, it is important that your cat is an inside cat, something that all owners should consider anyway since cats who roam only live an average of two to three years compared to inside cats who can live anywhere from 15 to 20 years.

Myth: A Cat is a Free Spirit Who Must be Free to Come and Go

Because cats give off an aura of independence and because they are more independent in nature than dogs, there is a persistent myth that says that cats need to be able to go outside when the desire strikes them.

Sure, given the choice, most cats would go outside if allowed. But that doesn't mean that cats should go outside. The outside world is a dangerous place for cats, with getting hit by a car being the number one way cats meet their demise. In addition, there are numerous airborne diseases that cats can easily catch from other cats, diseases that have no cures. And there is a very real threat of dying from attacks by other cats, dogs and other animals, and bites from snacks and poisonous frogs and insects.

Perhaps one of the biggest threats for outside cats is people. Cats are often the victim of cruelty at the hands of people who despise them, or they are taken by people who assume they do not belong to anyone.

Also, when cats roam, they can travel great distances and then wind up lost. Shelters are full of owned cats that were either found by people who brought them there or picked up by animal control officers. If an owner doesn't know to search the animal shelters or misses the arrival of their cat when searching there, then the cat can wind up either being adopted out to someone else or euthanized because of crowded conditions.

INTERVIEW WITH A HUMANE EDUCATOR:

Zoe Weil is the co-founder and president of the Institute for Humane Education located in Surry, ME, and is considered a pioneer in the comprehensive humane education movement. She is the author of six books and a writer of numerous articles on humane education and humane living. She is also a speaker and consultant on humane education, and serves on the board of directors of Humane Education Advocates Reaching Teachers (HEART).

What is the most difficult part of your job?

Simply getting the word out and garnering support for shifting the purpose of education from preparing students for global competitiveness to providing them with the knowledge, tools, and motivation to be solutionaries for a just, sustainable and humane world.

Why should people sterilize their cats?

To prevent an overpopulation problem that results in millions of healthy cats euthanized each year for lack of homes.

What are the benefits of adopting a cat from a shelter rather than a breeder?

By reducing demand for purchased and bred cats, we collectively limit the breeding of them. Plus you provide a home for an animal that might otherwise by euthanized.

Do you think Humane Education should be a part of a shelter's adoption program and why?

Absolutely. Humane education is the preventive work that will help reduce the numbers of unwanted animals in shelters and therefore reduce euthanasia. Without awareness and knowledge we cannot make informed, wise, compassionate choices. Moreover, humane education is good for everyone: it teaches about the interconnected issues of human rights, animal protection, and environmental sustainability, all necessary components of a just and peaceful world for all. Shelters have an important role to play in education.

Misconception: Cats Can Be Vegetarians

Cats are *obligate carnivores*, meaning that they must consume animal meat as part of their diet or their health will deteriorate. This is different from *carnivores*, such as humans and dogs, which are meat eaters who can extract protein from a vegetarian diet. Obligate carnivores *must* eat meat to survive. If you are a vegetarian or vegan for moral or health reasons, you cannot transfer this belief or eating style onto your cat without your feline paying the price with its health or even life.

That does not mean that cats can't eat fruit or vegetables. Just like humans, cats have individual tastes – one cat might love seafood, another hates it or prefers beef or chicken – and some actually enjoy the occasional fruit or veggie. But vegetation, while containing some amino acids, does not contain all of the amino acids that are critical for good feline health and therefore should not be a mainstay in a cat's diet. Also, unlike humans who can turn plant protein into amino acids, cats lack this ability.

In addition, a feline's unique body structure gets most if not all of its nutritional needs from the protein found solely in animal muscle. One of these necessary if not crucial amino acids that cats need to survive is Taurine, which if found primarily in the heart and liver. If a feline's diet lacks adequate amounts of Taurine, it can cause serious health problems, including cardiovascular disease and blindness. And should a human vegetarian think that all one needs to do is add a Taurine supplement to a cat's vegetarian diet, think again. As stated above, there are many types of amino acids only found in meat that cats must get through food. A multi vitamin for humans does not replace the natural vitamins and minerals found in real food any more than a Taurine supplement for cats would replace the vital nutrients cats must have on a daily basis that can only be found in animal tissue.

It is probably not a coincidence of nature that the domestication of cats started with them seeking out mice that were seeking out human stores of grain. The mouse is the perfect meat source for cats because mice contain the exact amount of amino acids, vitamins and minerals, as well as other nutritional needs, that felines require. They can, however, also carry disease, and since most human houses today are mice-free, it falls to humans to provide a healthy diet for their cats.

This means making sure that your feline's diet is free of carbohydrates, or at least includes only a minimal amount of carbs. This is because a cat's body is not designed to eat carbohydrates because cats do not produce the enzymes necessary to digest them. Humans and other plant eating omnivores or herbivores have a slower digestive system, which enables them to extract the nutrients and proteins they need from vegetation. But cats as obligate carnivores process food very quickly, so that food must be highly digestible and contain all the nutrients, vitamins and minerals necessary to maintain good health. Animal meat provides this.

One mistake some cat owners make is in thinking that they only need to feed their cats tuna. It's easy since it comes in a can and cats love it – in fact, given the choice, many cats would only opt for tuna. But this is not a balanced diet. For one thing, tuna is not nutritionally complete, is high in unsaturated fats, and can cause a vitamin E deficiency in your cat if fed a steady diet of tuna. This vitamin E deficiency can lead to *steatitis* or yellow fat disease, which is an inflammation of the fatty tissue and is very painful.

In addition, tuna is high in magnesium, which can increase your cat's susceptibility to urinary tract disease. Plus, many cats are allergic to fish, and like humans, can suffer if they consume too much mercury, which is found in most fish. The higher on the food chain a fish is, the higher amount of mercury is found in its tissue. Tuna has high amounts of mercury and, therefore, a steady diet of tuna leads to mercury poisoning. If your cat loves tuna, feed it cat food tuna rather than tuna canned for human consumption. Cat food tuna contains other ingredients, such as taurine, vitamins and minerals, so it is specially formatted for cats. But do not feed your cat this every day to avoid a buildup of mercury.

Commercial foods are the easiest means to provide your cat with its daily nutritional requirements. But some commercial foods are better than others, the best being those that have meat as its first ingredient rather than meat by-products, the latter of which is also cheaper. Some cat owners prefer feeding their pets a home prepared diet, while others feed their felines raw meat. It comes down to preference, costs and how much time you have to prepare your cat its food.

Whichever diet provisions you make for your cat, meat must be one of the ingredients and it must be high on the ingredient list – as nature intended. Otherwise, you could damage your cat's health and even contribute to its demise.

Myth: Female Cats Should Have One Litter Before They are Spayed, and Male Cats do Not Need to be Neutered

One only has to walk into an animal shelter and see the heart-breaking results of overpopulation. Cats are prolific breeders, and are capable of having three to four litters a year, with an average of three to four kittens per litter. Since only one feline in 12 will find a home, this leads to the death of over two million perfectly healthy cats unable to find homes at animal shelters each year.

Put another way, there are 10 homeless animals for each person living in the United States. A family of four would have to adopt 40 pets in order to provide homes for all of the homeless animals on the streets and languishing at shelters.

The overpopulation of cats is partially due to the procreation of feral cats, that is, cats born outside who are not owned and who have never learned the socialization skills necessary in order to become pets. But the biggest contributing factor to pet over-population is human failure to get their felines sterilized, either because of finances, lack of education about pet overpopulation, or misconceptions about why it is a necessary responsibility of cat ownership.

There are two contributing myths surrounding the sterilization of cats. One is that it is kind to permit a cat to have a litter of kittens before *spaying* – the procedure of sterilizing a female cat – and that the female will miss having a litter or feel sad about never being able to have kittens if not allowed to have at least one litter. This is incorrect on so many levels.

First, a cat who has never had a litter does not long to have a lit-ter the way a human female might long to have a baby. A com-mon mistake among pet owners is to inflict human sentiments on animals. While it is true that cats and other animals do share common emotions with people, such as sadness, happiness, love and loneliness, sexual feelings is not one of them. Humans have sex not just to procreate, but also to show love or desire for an-other human being. Cats have sex because instinct dictates that it is necessary in order for the species to survive.

Another excuse that humans use in allowing felines to have a litter is that they want their children to experience the miracle of birth. If this is true, then it is equally important to show children the devastation of death due to pet overpopulation. Statistics show that one female cat that is not sterilized can produce an average of three litters in one year. The average number of kittens in a litter is four to six, or 12 to 18 kittens a year. If each kitten is allowed to reproduce, the original female cat can be responsible for over 420,000 kittens over a seven year period! And since only one in 12 homeless cats find a home, it isn't hard to see why allowing your feline to reproduce is not just negligent, it is tragic.

The other part of this equation is the myth that if female cats are sterilized, it is then unnecessary to sterilize, or *neuter*, male cats. But a male cat on the prowl can impregnate an unlimited amount of intact females on any given day. In addition, male cats that are not sterilized tend to roam, and this territory can be quite extensive. This heightens the chances of your cat getting lost, taken by someone else who assumes he is a stray, hit by a car, contracting some of the many feline fatal diseases for which there are no cures, or being picked up by animal control or a person who takes him to an animal shelter where he may be adopted out to someone else or euthanized.

In addition, not sterilizing your cat lead can lead to behavior problems. Intact males tend to spray to mark their territories, which can damage other people's properties, or can ruin your furniture, carpet, shoes and other possessions in your home. And since intact males are territorial, this increases their chances of getting into fights with other males, which can lead to injuries, disease and even death.

Sterilization actually benefits a cat's health. Female cats that are spayed have a lower incidence of uterine, breast and ovarian cancer. In addition, spaying prevents pregnancy risks, including dying from complications while giving birth, and giving birth to deformed or stillborn kittens.

Male cats that have been neutered are less aggressive than intact males. The desire to mate is eliminated, a drive that can lead to fights, roaming dangers, and even bites. And despite the prevalent belief to the contrary, neutered males do not become lazy and overweight, the latter of which is usually the result of overfeeding, too many treats, and a lack of playful exercise. Spayed and neutered cats also live longer lives.

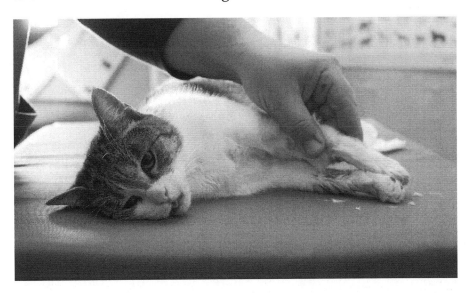

The best age to spay or neuter your cat is about four to six months of age, when cats reach sexual maturity and are larger and stronger when put under general anesthesia. This is because the smaller the animal, the greater the stress on the heart and the greater the chance of complications during surgery. Older cats in good health are also good candidates for sterilization. However, most animal shelters will perform sterilization on kittens as young as eight weeks of age, as well as older cats, because of the high incidence of adopters who never bring their cats back for the procedure. Sterilizing kittens and cats before adoption helps to battle the tragedy of overpopulation by eliminating the possibility of those cats reproducing once they have left the shelter.

Of course there is another side of the spay-neuter argument. Most cats are mixed breeds, also known as domestic short-, medium- and long-haired cats, a name given to felines that do not belong to a specific breed or are purebred. But there are 41 pedigreed or purebred breeds that are recognized by *Cat Fanciers Association*, which is the largest registry of pedigreed cats in the United States. And some put the number of breeds much higher on a worldwide scale.

May cat breeders argue that they keep the different cat breeds pure and that they continue the linage of breeds that go back hundreds and even thousands of years. While this statement is true, there is also the argument that there is no guarantee that the offspring of purebreds that are sold will not wind up mating with mixed breeds and therefore add to the overpopulation problem.

The truth is, 20 percent of animals at animal shelters are pure-breds. Just because a buyer spends hundreds of dollars on a specific breed of cat is no guarantee that that cat will not at some point in time wind up abandoned. Also, because money is also a factor in cat breeding, this has resulted in the proliferation of backyard breeders who do not have the proper genetics knowledge of what is involved in keeping a breed pure, or the training needed to make sure a purebred cat is not over bred, resulting in sick or deformed offspring or offspring that are too closely related which can lead to health problems and genetic mutations.

Some animal welfare groups argue that the way to cut out the backyard breeder is to require that professional breeders purchase a license to breed each year and open their facilities up for inspection to make sure they are not operating what is known as a *kitten mill*, breeding places that are known for horrendous conditions and over breeding. Unfortunately, most breeders have successfully fought such regulations, even though these procedures could help to ensure purity of the breed and the integrity of their profession.

If you are thinking of becoming a breeder, keep in mind that this is not a get-rich-quick field. Breeding purebred cats is expensive in terms of the time and money involved in caring for kittens and adult cats. In addition, breeders face the same challenges that animal shelters do – not enough homes to go around. Most professional breeders do it for the love of a particular breed and the desire to keep that breed in existence and pure, not because the financial rewards are great.

Outside of professional breeding, most cat owners will find that a sterilized feline is more enjoyable to have around than one that is driven by sexual procreation. A sterilized cat has no desire to roam or spray, is less aggressive, less restless, and healthier, and in the long run, less likely to die of cancer and other diseases.

Myth: Cats are a Danger to Pregnant Women

One of the oldest myths about cats that persists to this day is that cats can harm pregnant women. This is because there is a very real danger of contracting *Toxoplasmosis*, a condition caused by a parasite known as *Toxoplasma gondii*, which can cause miscarriages or birth defects in fetuses whose mothers are exposed to it during pregnancy. And while it is true that some cats are carriers through the parasite eggs in cat feces, the parasite that carries this disease is found more often in infected soil that you can come in contact with when you are digging in your garden, and when handling raw or undercooked meat.

If you allow your cats to go outside, they can come in contact this with this disease-carrying parasite, which they then shed via their feces in their litter boxes. The simple solution is not to get rid of your cat, but to have someone else scoop the waste matter instead, or to wear rubber gloves when handling the litter box. The better solution is to keep your cats indoors as inside cats.

A poor solution is to get rid of your cat if you or someone in your family is pregnant. Unfortunately, this myth is still one reason why cats are given up at animal shelters, either because of lack of knowledge on the owner's part or because their doctor also believes this inaccuracy and has advised them to give up their cat.

It is equally important to avoid stray cats if you are pregnant, since many also carry Toxoplasmosis from eating birds, rodents and other small animals that have the parasites inside them. They then shed the parasite in dirt or soil, which is why it is important to wear gloves when gardening.

When it comes to your own cat, do not feed it raw or undercooked meat if you are pregnant. Stick to commercial cat food during this time. It is also important to remember that a cat's feces is only infectious for one to five days before the parasitic egg spores die, which means your cat's poop would have to sit in the litter box for this length of time – and not too many cats will put up with that kind of neglect before finding another place to eliminate.

If you or a pregnant family member wants to play it entirely safe, get someone else to do the scooping or get a self-cleaning litter box that places feces in a bag ready to be put in the trash. If you are doing the scooping, wear gloves and always wash your hands afterwards. Whatever you do, do not get rid of your cat. It is an unnecessary and heartbreaking course of action to take.

Myth: Cats are a Danger to Babies and Should Never be Around Them

An age old myth that seems preposterous yet persists today is that a cat will willingly and knowingly kill or harm a baby. One such persistent story is that a cat will steal a baby's breath or suck the life out of a baby. This old wives' tale may be based on the habit of cats to seek out warmth and comfort, and when cuddling in a baby's crib, this could cause snuggling next to a baby's face. If a baby is too young to turn away, the cat pressing near his or her face might cause the baby to die from SIDS or *Sudden Infant Death Syndrome*, a syndrome where it is believed that a baby suffocates and dies because the baby's breathing stops or something hampers the breathing. Perhaps the origin of this myth lies in the past, when SIDS, as it was once called, Crib Death, occurred and a cat may have been blamed because of its close proximity to the baby at the time, or because the cat was lying next to the baby's face causing the baby to smother, causing people to believe that the cat had actually stolen the baby's breath.

In any case, it is imperative that you keep your baby's door closed when he or she is napping, in order to prevent any harm to the baby as the result of your cat's curiosity about this new addition to the family.

It is equally important to make your baby's room off limits to your cat, and to only allow your cat around your baby under supervision. Under your watchful gaze, you should allow your cat to smell the baby so that your feline becomes familiar with this new addition and doesn't feel displaced. If your cat seems apprehensive, do not force the issue. Welcome your cat to sit next to you when you are holding your baby, so that your pet can become accustomed to the new smells and sounds.

You can help to make the transition of having a baby in the house easier for your cat by preparing your feline for the baby prior to the newborn's arrival. One way is to put baby powder or baby lotion on your skin and let your cat smell it, so that once the baby arrives, your cat is familiar with these scents. You can also play a recording of baby sounds prior to the baby's birth, so that once your baby is here, your cat is used to these sounds.

Another important thing to do is to give your cat undivided attention once the baby arrives. Cats, like people, feel jealousy, rejection and hurt feelings, especially if your feline is used to getting attention and then suddenly is ignored.

Also make sure to keep your cat's nails trimmed. Babies reach out and grab, which can be painful to your feline should your baby grasp tightly to your cat's tail or ears. A cat's natural defense is to lash out and scratch. The longer and sharper the claws, the higher the chances are of wounding your baby and maybe even permanently scaring him or her.

If your baby is a toddler, he or she might hug your cat too tightly when expressing affection for your feline. This also could cause your cat to scratch or even bite out of pain. Always supervise any interaction between your baby or toddler and your cat to prevent accidental wounding or pain. Do not admonish or punish your cat if he or she acts out or is upset by your baby. Instead, be sensitive to your cat's confusion and pile on the love and understanding. By keeping an eye on the activity between your baby and your cat, you can forge a deep and loving relationship between the two that can last for many years.

Sadly, many cats go from being a member of the family to being turned over to a shelter or put outside to live once a baby arrives. This is not just cruel to your cat because it will feel abandoned and confused, but it can also be a threat to its life since it may be euthanized at an animal shelter or may wind up injured, killed or starved to death if left to fend for itself outside. A few simple preparations can make life with baby and cat an easy and happy transition. By keeping an eye on the activity between your baby and your cat, you can forge a deep and loving relationship between the two that can last for many years.

Misconception: Cats Should be Free to Come and Go

Given the choice, most cats would prefer to be indoor/outdoor cats, free to come and go as they please. But that doesn't mean they should be or need to be, or that you are keeping your feline a prisoner by not giving them this freedom.

While it is true that if you adopt an older cat who has spent its life being an outside or inside/outside cat, you might have a difficult time keeping this cat happy as an indoor-only cat, most cats adjust quite well to living entirely indoors. In fact, it is better for them.

Cats who are allowed to freely roam live an average of two to four years, compared to cat who live entirely inside can live an average of 15 to 20 years. This is because danger lurks in many ways for cats who are allowed to roam and these very real hazards contribute to the deaths of thousands of felines each year.

The number one way outdoor cats die is by being hit by cars. Cats do not comprehend the risks of approaching cars or know how to avoid busy streets, and often run out into traffic. Cats can also be eaten by coyotes and other animals, or be killed by dogs roaming free. Felines can also wind up trapped in other people's sheds, garages and basements, where if undetected over a long period of time can lead to death from dehydration or starvation.

Cats have been known to hide under car hoods when the weather is cold, leading to terrible and painful injuries or death when the owner starts the car. They are poisoned from weed killers and fertilizers used on lawns and antifreeze that has leaked from engines, which has a sweet appealing taste, or they are poisoned from eating rodents that have ingested poison. Outdoor cats often suffer from flea infestation, undetected parasites, and insect bites. Fights with other cats can lead to injuries or even death, and they can contract untreatable and incurable diseases that are spread airborne or via bites from other cats. Cats can also suffer from injuries incurred when they climb and fall out of trees or attempt to jump from a tree branch or a balcony wall that is too high off the ground. Contrary to popular belief, cats do not always land on their feet and often suffer from broken bones or even death when jumping down to the ground from high places.

In addition to safety and health reasons, keeping your cat indoors can also prevent bad neighborly relations. Cats who are free to roam can stir up barking among nearby dogs, dig up your neighbor's garden and flowers, stalk and kill songbirds at a rate of millions a year, and cause hard to get rid of stenches by spraying your neighbor's fence, house and yard. Despite what many people believe, many towns and cities have ordinances that state that your feline is not free to come and go wherever they want if they are a nuisance to your neighbors. This could lead to a neighbor trapping and taking your cat to an animal shelter or worse, poisoning your cat – which is against the law but hard to prove.

If you raise a cat from kittenhood or young adulthood to be an inside cat, or you adopt an older cat who has always lived indoors, your cat will be perfectly happy and often prefer to live its life inside the safety of your home. That doesn't mean there isn't a downside. Indoor cats are often overweight from being overfed and from lack of exercise. Owners who aren't willing to or aren't able to spend time playing with their cats can cause boredom, frustration and bad behavior or bad habits among their felines.

The trick is keeping your indoor cat happy and free from boredom, as well as play that involves moving about, and that requires a little effort. On the top of this list is adopting more than one cat. Just like people, cats are happiest when they have a feline companion or even a dog companion. Even if the two cats or your cat and dog never become "best buds," it is still comforting to your cats to have another pet in the mix, someone who to keep them company during those times when you're out of the house.

You should also provide your cat with plenty of toys that are designed for fun and intellectual stimulation. A simple ball batted across the floor, a string or toy hanging from a door knob, a box to hide inside of, a squeaky toy or moving toy, can all provide hours of enjoyment. Try to rotate the toys, since cats, like people, can become bored with the same toy. Also, make sure to play with your inside kitty. Games like the device that shines a red dotted light on the floor that a cat can pounce on when moved are a favorite among many felines. Or take a string or rope and run with it. Your cat will chase it in an attempt to grab it. Fake mice, especially those that contain catnip, are also popular toys because they appeal to your cat's natural instinct to stalk and hunt. And since cats love to hide, a good old cardboard box or a paper bag (not plastic!) or a kitty tent can provide hours of entertainment.

Scratching posts are also an important item to provide for your indoor feline. Cats need to sharpen and shorten their claws, as well as mark territory through scent glands located on their paws, and will find whatever is available in order to do this natural activity. This is not a problem when they go outside, but indoor cats will use whatever is available, such as your couch, curtains and carpet. If you provide a scratching post that stands at least two feet tall, however, they will choose this over your furniture and drapes. It is important, however, to have at least one scratching post in each room. A cat that is upstairs or in another room and has the urge to scratch, won't take the time to locate the post that's in one room; it will simply find what is readily available, such as your furniture. Make the scratch post more attractive by rubbing catnip on it.

Another way to keep your indoor cat happy is to make sure there are several windows that can be gazed out of. Cats love to watch birds fly and move about, as well as trees blowing in the breeze or people walking by, and will spend hours staring out the window. Think of it as TV for cats. Feline eyes can detect the slightest movements, so make it easy by also providing some kind of perch and place it in front of a window. If possible, place a birdbath outside where your cat can spend hours of enjoyment watching the birds come and go. Perches are also great because cats love to be in high places where they can look down on people and other pets.

An ideal way to keep your indoor cat happy is to allow it to go out on a patio or to build a screened walkway that leads to an enclosed area outside. This can help to alleviate the guilt felt by owners of indoor cats that they are not providing their cats with fresh air and sunshine.

Another alternative – if your feline will tolerate it – is to walk your cat on a cat leash attached to a harness or collar. Most cats do not like being pulled on a collar, so a harness provides a freer feeling. If you have a fenced in yard or patio, you might allow your cat to run about – provided you keep a close eye on your feline and that the fence is high. Cats can jump great heights and will if that provides an escape.

Don't forget to provide your indoor cat with plenty of veggies. One enticement about the great outdoors is the grass and other natural vegetation to chomp down on. You can counter this by growing cat grass, which is actually oat seedlings, that your feline can chew on when the mood strikes. Also, provide catnip if your cat likes it – not all do – to eat or roll around in.

If you do decide that it is best to allow your cat the freedom to go outside, then make sure it is microchipped so that if it gets lost, the person or shelter who finds it is able to determine who your cat belongs to. Also, make sure your feline wears a collar with its rabies tag and your phone number displayed. Many people are unaware of microchipping and this is added insurance that you will get your cat back. In addition, make sure the collar is a "break-away" kind, so that if it gets caught on a bush or some other item, the cat won't strangle or be injured. Also, make sure your cat is up-to-date on vaccines in case it crosses path with a rabid or diseased animal, although this will not prevent your cat from contracting one of the many diseases that have no vaccines or cures.

Another thing to be aware of is that outdoor cats or cats that are allowed to roam are in danger of being victims of animal cruelty. Cats have been victims of BB gun shots or regular gun shots, bows and arrows, torture, trapping, and killed for sport, or for a sport, such as bait for illegal dog fighting. In addition, there are people who drive around neighborhoods called *bunchers*, who pick up strays and owned cats and sell them to laboratories to be used in animal testing and experiments. Many laboratories do not have to account for where or who they purchased their animals from, so selling to these facilities is easy money.

Never, ever let a declawed cat venture outside, especially if you are not around to supervise the experience. Cats that are declawed have no way to defend themselves against other cats, dogs and other animals. Some declawed cats become biters, but this is rarely an equal defense mechanism when up against another cat's claws or a larger animal's teeth. Plus, in many towns and cities, biting another animal can equal a trip for your cat to the animal shelter for quarantine where your feline may have to spend ten days being observed for signs of rabies.

The bottom line is, indoors is best and outdoors is hazardous. If your cat has always been an outdoor cat and you know want to make it an indoor feline, you need to make indoor life interesting. It's as simple as that. Many an outdoor cat has happily become an indoor cat. Doing so not only keeps your feline safe for the many reasons already mentioned, but it also gives you the peace of mind of not having to worry if your kitty is safe or coming home.

Myth: Cats Always Land on Their Feet

Cats have a unique body that can recoil for jumping up and twist when jumping or falling down in order to land of their feet. But that does not mean every fall is successful and without injuries.

Cats can survive long falls, but sometimes this can result in broken bones or internal injuries. New York City veterinarians use the term, *High Rise Syndrome*, for injuries cats incur when falling out of windows from high rise buildings. Supposedly, the record of survival for a cat falling from a high rise is 18 stories, but that doesn't mean you shouldn't be aware of keeping windows closed if you live in a home with more than one story. Your cat might be able to land on its feet from a long fall, but the fall can result in broken bones and other serious injuries to its legs and chest, or even death. Ironically, a shorter fall of 10 to 12 feet can also cause a cat to sustain injuries. To understand why, you first have to understand what happens to a cat's body when it goes into freefall.

When cats fall, the fluid in their inner ears will shift, causing the cat to rotate its head in order to level this fluid. This, combined with its flexible spine that is able to quickly twist while at the same time counter rotating its tail to stabilize the fall, causes a cat's body to shift or upright its position in order to follow the head. As this is occurring, the cat will arch its back away from its legs while extending those legs in preparation of landing. These actions occurring in a falling cat's body all come together at nearly the same time, enabling the cat to land on its feet where the pads on its paws act like a shock absorber. But when a cat falls a shorter distance of 10 to 12 feet (or less), there often isn't enough time for the cat to spring around and land feet first because it can take about 10 feet in midair for this fine acrobatic action to come together and prepare for landing.

Falls, in fact, are one of the main reasons why cats wind up in veterinary emergency rooms. If your cat falls out of a window or off your balcony, or if your cat appears to be in pain or is limping, take it to your vet right away. It could have a broken bone or internal injuries that are impossible to detect without x-rays. Be careful handling a cat you think may be inured. Animals in pain are more liable to lash out.

Myth: Cats and Dogs Don't Get Along

Although many people view dogs and cats as enemies or believe that a dog will always chase or attack a cat, there are many blended families where cats and dogs either enjoy each other's company or at least tolerate their co-existence in relative peace. In fact, most dogs like cats; it's the cats that are more leery of dogs.

It depends on the cat, of course. And perhaps more importantly, it depends on the dog. There are some breeds or types of dogs that are called high prey dogs, the type who would go after a squirrel or rabbit. These dogs have a natural hunting instinct and will automatically go after a cat. There are also dogs who might chase cats, squirrels and other small animals outside, but who tolerate or even like the cat or cats that live with them.

Cats that grow up with dogs usually don't have a problem being around non aggressive or non hunting type dogs. There are
many love bonds between cats and dogs that defy this common
belief that they are enemies. Some cats will accept the dog they
live with, but may be afraid of a new dog they encounter. If your
cat is meeting a new dog member of the family, it is important
to introduce them slowly. Also, this introduction should be over
a period of time and not something that is rushed. This will prevent any aggressive behavior or fearful feelings that can mar the
relationship for the long run.

Start by confining your feline to one room, regardless of whether
your cat is the resident pet, that is, was there first, or if it is a new
cat you are bringing into the family. Make sure you place a litter
box and food and water, as well as comfort toys and a comfy bed
or place to sleep, in the room.

Next, feed your cat on one side of the door and your dog on the
other. This way, they will get used to each other's smells and associate being near each other with something pleasurable such
as eating.

Then see if you can get your cat and dog to interact while playing. Start by tying a toy on each end of a string, and slide this
under the door so that your cat has one toy on its side of the door,
and your dog as another toy on its side. This should lead to each
pet batting its toy and maybe even playing "paws" with each
other under the door.

**Remember: smells should always be the meet-and-greet before
your cat and dog meet face-to-face.** If your dog has slept on a
blanket, you might want to move that blanket into the room your
cat is confined in to allow it to get used to the dog's scent. You
can also wipe a wash cloth on the cat's face and then let the dog

smell it, or visa versa. This exchange of scents will accomplish the same thing and when your cat and dog finally meet, they will be familiar with each other's smells. And you can turn the encounter into a positive experience by giving your cat treats while the dog is sitting in the same room. Also, be sure your dog is trained enough to listen to your commands and reinforce its good behavior around the cat through dog treats and praise.

On a positive note, cats usually don't view dogs as competition the way they view new cats. Cats that have lived in multi-cat families also tend to be less stressed by the addition of a dog and may even find the dog intriguing or will watch the dog from a distance until it can be sure the dog is not a threat.

It's important to be patient, however, because cats are not as trusting as dogs. It can take weeks, months or even years for a trust and bond to form between your cat and dog. It helps if your cat is young or if your dog is a puppy or a small breed and, therefore, appears less threatening to your cat. But like people, sometimes a cat meets a dog and they just click. Sometimes, it is not the cat that is afraid of your dog; it is the dog that is cautious about the cat. Your dog, particularly an older dog, might go out of its way to avoid your cat or will keep its distance from your cat. Whatever the case, it is very important to never leave a dog and cat together unsupervised until you know for sure that they like or at least tolerate each other enough to be safe when you are not around. And if your cat is fearful or wants to retreat, always give it the space and ability to do so.

Also, make sure that your dog does not have access to your cat's litter box. Cats are very particular about their boxes and having a dog disrupt that could cause additional stress. Feeding your cat in another room or at a higher level such as a counter or cat perch can also alleviate your cat's stress or mistrust and keep your dog from eating the cat's food or drinking its water.

If you allow your cat to befriend your dog on the cat's terms, you can help to forge a peaceful, happy and even loving bond. At the very least, you will create an environment where the cat views the dog as another family member it doesn't mind tolerating.

Misconception: Cats Are Not as Affectionate as Dogs

One of the biggest misconceptions about cats is that they are not affectionate the way dogs are, and are aloof, unfeeling creatures. But anyone who has ever shared their lives with a cat will tell you that cats give people as much love as dogs do – without the wet licks.

Cats are often used as therapy animals at nursing homes and in some hospitals because of their calm demeanor and purring that can actually lower stress levels. Many cats will greet their owners at the door, sleep with people, and even "clean" a person by licking in the same manner as they do when they are cleaning themselves. Many a cat will curl up to nap on its person's lap, and can become depressed when its owner dies. Cats, like dogs, are in tune with their owner's feelings and some will comfort their people through purring and snuggling. And cats have been known to get sick or depressed if ignored by their owners or if their people do not have the time to give them attention. Many a cat abandoned at an animal shelter will get ill from depression and die. This is only possible if a cat can feel affection.

Like dogs, cats are also affectionate with the cats and dogs that live with them. Cats will often spend time licking or cleaning each other, and some cats will even "clean" the dog. When a person or another pet dies, cats have been known to go into deep depression, an emotion that can only be felt by an affectionate animal.

The misconception about cats not being as affectionate as dogs may stem from the fact cats are not as demonstrative as dogs, that is, they do not have that wagging tail that signals happiness, they don't slobber all over their owners with wet licks, or leap up on hind legs to greet their people. Cats have other ways to show affection, their own language if you will. Knowing what that language is will not only disprove this misconception, it will also grow the bonds between you and your cat.

One way a cat shows love is by rubbing against you, curling its tail around your leg or arm, and walking in and out of your legs. When your cat does this, it is claiming you as its person or marking you as its property. It is also a form of greeting you, such as when you first get up in the morning or come home after being home for the day or night.

Sometimes a cat will touch you with its nose, either on your nose or mouth or on a part of your body, or smell your face and then touch your face with its nose. This is a form of cat kiss, an affectionate gesture that signals she likes you and feels comfortable around you. Another type of cat kissing is when a cat stares at you and then slowly blinks. This is also a cat kiss. Often, if you blink back, your cat will blink again or if you blink first, your cat will then blink. This is the ultimate display of trust, since it is not uncommon for a new cat or an unfamiliar cat to stare and not blink if you try this cat kiss on them.

When a cat head-butts you, that is rubs its head hard on you, it is showing affection and friendliness. A cat's head rub is an ultimate, "I love you." A cat will also knead you with its front paws in a way similar to how a kitten kneads its mother's nipples when nursing. Cat kneading is done rhythmically, with one paw pressing and then the other, alternating from one paw then the other back and forth, usually in conjunction with purring. This display means that your cat trusts you and is a sign of happiness, contentment or playfulness.

Cat grooming is another way your feline will show its love and affection. Your cat may try to eat your hair or will lick and clean between each of your fingers. This means your cat considers you its family and is similar to what mother cats do to their kittens. You can return the favor by petting your feline, especially around the head, cheeks and under the chin. For your cat, petting is a form of grooming which translates into affection, plus it feels good to your cat.

Some cats give love bites as a sign of affection. But if the bite is hard and hurts, this can also mean that your cat is over stimulated and wants the petting or attention to stop.

Perhaps the best known and most familiar sign of affection is when a cat purrs. This usually means a cat is happy and content. It should be noted, however, that cats also purr when they are depressed or sick, as it is a way that they comfort themselves.

These displays of affection are a compliment. They mean your cat is emotionally connected to you. Cats will also use these affectionate body gestures with other cats and dogs in your home. Some cats are very affectionate, while others are less so. But this is no different than people, some of whom are very huggy and kissy, while other people are more reserved. The trick is to learn your cat's affectionate language and then build on it. It will deepen the bonds between you.

Silly Superstitions That Persist to This Day

Whiskers give a cat balance

One superstition claims that if you cut off a cat's whiskers, it will lose its balance. But a cat's whiskers have absolutely nothing to do with balance, although they are essential.

Whiskers are, in fact, touch receptors. Whiskers, also called *vibrissae*, are actually hair that is stronger, stiffer and thicker than say the hair that makes up a cat's fur. Their purpose is to send signals to the cat's sensory nerves, enabling the cat to detect changes in and information about a cat's surroundings.

Cats have an average of 24 whiskers in four rows on their muzzles. Each one is moveable, with the top rows moving independently of the bottom rows. Whiskers are embedded deep into the cat, attaching to a cat's sensory and nervous systems and work like a type of radar system that sends images to the brain. The most prevalent place to find whiskers is on each side of your cat's nose and upper lip in the puffy area of its face, but whiskers are also located above each eye, sort of like kitty eyebrows, as well as on the jaw line and back of each front leg.

Cutting off a cat's whiskers is harmful, but not because of balance. If a cat loses its whiskers, it can disorient it and prevent it from gauging and making sense of its surroundings. Although whiskers will grow back, cutting them would be similar to you losing your sense of touch. Whiskers not only send signals to a cat about its environment, they can help a cat get around in the dark and alert it to dangerous or painful situations.

This is done through the *proprioceptor*, a sensory organ located on the tips of the whiskers that sends signals to a cat's brain and nervous system. The proprioceptor helps the cat to be aware of even the most minute changes in its surroundings, and can help a cat decide whether or not it can fit into a tight space, which is the primary reason why cats have whiskers. Think of whiskers as a type of kitty ruler that protects your cat from getting stuck since whiskers tend to be the same width as your cat's body. When you witness your cat sticking its head in and out of an opening before going into an enclosed area, it is using its whiskers as an indicator of whether or not the space is one it can fit into.

Whiskers also help a cat pick up vibrations in the air, such as the vibrations created by the size and shape of an object, such as when a cat is going after prey. This sensory organ on the whiskers can help a cat to measure distance when leaping up on a higher level or away from danger. It is said that whiskers are so sensitive, they can pick up a change in air direction. Air direction, for cats, sends signals about what is in its environment. This is how a cat is able to walk into a dark room and not trip or bump into anything. This is partly due to a cat's ability to see better in the dark than humans, but it is also due to its whiskers.

Whiskers also indicate a cat's mood. A cat at peace will have immobile whiskers, but one that is scared may have whiskers that lay flat across its face or are bunched together. When a cat is chasing a toy or is in hunting mode, its whiskers often point forward. And when a cat is startled or is excited, its whiskers will stand up and forward in the same way as its fur stands on end.

It is suggested that your cat bowls be wide and flat, or at least be a bowl that is as wide as your cat's whiskers. Felines hate it when their whiskers touch the sides of their bowls. It feels uncomfortable and irritating.

Cats do shed their whiskers. There's another superstition that says that when you find a whisker, which you will occasionally, you should make a wish. But this is done one at a time, usually because a new one is growing in its place. The cat does not miss the whisker the way it would if you were to trim or cut off all of its whiskers at one time. Cut whiskers will grow back, but the procedure is detrimental to cat's well being.

Cats have nine lives

Perhaps there was a time when this superstition seemed to make sense to people. It probably stems from witnessing a cat's resilient nature and ability to often escape danger. Some experts theorize that this myth could go all the way back to ancient Egypt where it was believed that the Sun god, Atum-Ra, one of the Nine or nine gods, would don the head of a cat when visiting the underworld, making nine a mystical number. This belief in a cat's nine lives had continued through the ages probably due to cats' seemingly mysterious and even magical nature.

Today, most people would agree that cats do not have nine lives. Yet many people mistakenly believe that cats are almost invincible, as discussed earlier, such as in the assumption that a cat will always land on its feet in a fall. Also, many cat owners assume that cats can dodge in and out of traffic, or that felines have enough sense to know when traffic is too busy and not to cross the street. This flies in the face of thousands of cat deaths each year from being hit by cars, as well as death from injuries sustained from falling.

What cats can do, however, is experience nine emotions: fear, anticipation, anxiety, depression, grief, happiness, love, dislike and pleasure. Some of these emotions are long term, since cats have long memories and can remember if an activity or experience is frightful or fun. The love that cats have for their owners is also long term, as is depression and grief. But some cat emotions are in the moment, such as when a cat leaps and misses its target. Cats are capable of feeling humiliation, but that won't stop the cat from making the leap again. You could say that perhaps the idea of nine lives stems from these nine emotions that demonstrate that a cat is an intelligent, feeling and deeply sensitive animal who is also a survivor.

Cats are nocturnal

This superstition may stem from the belief that cats can see better in the dark due to their eye structure that allows them to see in low light levels and, therefore, must be nocturnal. Both assumptions are incorrect. While it is true that a cat can see better in dark circumstances than humans do, this does not mean they have night vision, only that their eyes can detect objects in lower light settings with more ease than the human eye. Nor does it mean that cats want to be up in the middle of the night, as evidenced by many cat owners who enjoy their cats snuggling next to them while sleeping.

Cats spend two thirds of their lives sleeping, but that does not mean they're up all night. In fact, cats *crepuscular*, meaning they are programmed to hunt at dawn and dusk, not in the middle of the night. Most indoor cats are crepuscular, so they tend to sleep at night and take cat naps during the day.

Outdoor cats are often both nocturnal and *diurnal*, meaning that some outdoor cats *are* active at night when temperatures are cooler, while others are active during the day, making them diurnal. And most indoor cats do tend to get active at bedtime, almost as if they get a second wind. But they are not up all night, as true nocturnal animals are.

Cat owners often reinforce this nighttime activity, however. A cat might bug its owner to be fed in the middle of the night and in order to get some sleep, the owner gets up and feeds the cat. This reinforces the behavior and it becomes a vicious cycle. You can break this bad habit by playing with your cat during the day and feeding it during set daytime hours. Your cat will be exhausted by bedtime and will need to sleep through the night in order to get its 16 hours of beauty sleep.

For cat owners who are at work all day, this might prove to be a little more difficult. The main reason why cats wake us in the middle of the night or early in the morning is because they are hungry. You can remedy the situation by feeding your cat its largest meal right before bedtime, with smaller meals during the day. Also, leave plenty of toys around so that your cat gets plenty of exercise and is ready then to settle in for the night. You can also try keeping your bedroom door closed if your cat tends to wake you during the night. But this is not always an option, since many a cat knows that a persistent meow or a paw under the door jiggling it back and forth is enough to make an exasperated owner get up and open it.

Most indoor cats tend to follow the schedules of their owners, particularly if those owners are around. Cats are great adapters and will adapt their sleeping schedules to those of their humans. Still, most cats do wake up several times during the night, and will also change sleeping areas throughout the night. If you awaken to a cat batting a ball or running around, your cat is simply displaying its natural crepuscular tendencies.

Cats hate water

Cats have a love/hate relationship with water. Most cats hate baths, but some don't mind it. However, when it comes to running water, cats are fascinated by it and many cats prefer to drink out of a running faucet as opposed to the still water in a bowl.

It is necessary to bathe your cat every once in a while, despite a cat's ability to bathe or clean itself. A cat can start to smell from its saliva after awhile, and a bath can make its fur softer, smell better, and alleviate any dry skin or other irritations. The trick is, getting your cat to take a bath without it turning into a hissing, clawing feat.

If your cat is small, you might be able to bathe it in the kitchen sink. This is perfect also if you have a kitten because it can get used to the idea of having a bath once in a while. But if your cat is larger, a bath tub is better because it is harder for it to grip its claws on the slippery bottom. Wear gloves and get someone to help, if need be. One person can flank the cat over the arm so that it's hard for the cat to gain traction and escape, while the other person can pour the water and suds up the fur. It is extremely important to always use shampoo that is made for cats. Human shampoo can make a cat sick and maybe even kill it.

Also, make sure your cat always has fresh water to drink. Cats are not always in love with the taste of water and are notorious for being dehydrated. When they do drink, they prefer cold, fresh water or as mentioned, water right from the tap. But if you notice your cat is drinking an abnormal amount of water – or more water than usual – take it into the vet. Inability to quench thirst can indicate cat diabetes or cat hyperthyroid disease.

Black cats are unlucky

It is an age old superstition that black cats are unlucky, some people today are wary of black cats. It's a myth these felines can't shake. The origin of the unlucky black cat is its link to pagan times when cats were often worshipped in various pagan religions. As Christianity spread across Europe, the black cat became vilified as a symbol of pagan evil.

But it was Pope Gregory IX who in 1233 ACE who singled the black cat out as the devil incarnated. Christians followed this pope's directive and gathered up all black cats they could find and burned them alive. The devastation was so great that by the 14th century, black cats were extinct in some parts of Europe.

It was long after that the jump was made to link black cats to witches. Black cats were labeled *familiars*, rather, the withes themselves in disguise. Some people also believed that black cats could turn themselves into witches. During the 16th and 17th centuries, which witnessed hundreds of people being put on trial for the crime of witchcraft, owning a black cat was evidence enough to be arrested and put to death for being a witch.

Ironically, in some parts of the world, including Great Britain and Japan, black cats are considered lucky. But the hysteria over witchcraft in most of Europe and the black cat's association with the devil, sorcery and bad luck has mostly been devastating to many black cat populations.

Sadly, this apprehension of black cats continue to this day, as evidenced by the fact that black cats have the most difficult time being adopted at animal shelters compared to other cats of other colors. Given the fact that 70 percent of cats at animal shelters are eventually euthanized, having a black coat gives a homeless cat an extra strike against it.

Cats are mean, sneaky and untrustworthy

People who don't understand cats or that are avid dog lovers often classify cats as mean, sneaky, manipulative and untrustworthy, cold and aloof creatures that are incapable of loyalty and love. As any cat lover will tell you, however, nothing could be further from the truth.

While it is true that cats don't wag their tails, lick faces, and demonstrate other demonstrative forms of affection the way dogs do, cats do have a wide array of emotions, can be very attached to their owners, and show their affection in more quiet ways.

In fact, one reason why cats can make great therapy cats is that they are affectionate and friendly. They also display this friendliness to strangers who enter your home by rubbing against them or sitting in their laps. In fact, it is an ironic tendency for cats to make a beeline right to the person in the room who professes that they hate cats or are afraid of cats. Perhaps cats obtain a sixth sense if you will, being able to intuitively pick out those humans who are good people, regardless of whether or not they like cats? Or maybe it's a cat's way of trying to win over those with little understanding or affection for cats. In addition, cats show affection time and again to other family cats or other pets.

Perhaps it is a cat's intelligence that often leads it to be classified as sneaky and manipulative. A cat is willing to obey the rules, but sometimes its desire to obtain something or be in a certain location can lead it to go after what it wants when you are not around – such as leaping on to the kitchen counter or sleeping in a room that you don't allow it to enter. What appears as sneakiness is really an example of a cat's intelligence and curiosity. Say no to a cat and it wants to know why. But as any pet owner who has set up a camera to record the actions of its pets when that owner isn't around will tell you, dogs also get up to things they know are against the rules when their owners are home.

In any case, attempting to force a dog's traits and personality on a cat is to disrespect the unique, loving and intelligent traits of most cats. Besides, if cats really were mean, sneaky and manipulative they would not now be the most popular pet in the world.

INTERVIEW WITH A HUMANE EDUCATOR:

Zoe Weil is the co-founder and president of the Institute for Humane Education (IHE) located in Surry, ME. She is considered a pioneer in the comprehensive humane education movement, and is the author of six books, Most Good, Least Harm: A Simple Principle for a Better World and Meaningful Life. She has also written numerous articles on humane education and humane living, and has given interviews to Forbes.com and numerous radio and television stations.

Ms. Weil speaks about humane education and humane living at universities, conferences and schools, and communities across the United States and Canada and periodically overseas. She has also served as a consultant on humane education to people and organizations around the world, and serves on the board of directors of Humane Education Advocates Reaching Teachers (HEART). For more information about IHE and humane education certification programs, go to **www.humaneeducation.org**.

What is the most difficult part of your job?

Simply getting the word out and garnering support for shifting the purpose of education from preparing students for global competitiveness to providing them with the knowledge, tools, and motivation to be solutionaries for a just, sustainable and humane world.

Why should people sterilize their cats?

To prevent an overpopulation problem that results in millions of healthy cats euthanized each year for lack of homes.

What are the benefits of adopting a cat from a shelter rather than a breeder?

By reducing demand for purchased and bred cats, we collectively limit the breeding of them and limit the overpopulation epidemic. Plus you provide a home for an animal who might otherwise be euthanized.

Do you think Humane Education should be a part of a shelter's adoption program and why?

Absolutely. Humane education is the preventive work that will help reduce the numbers of unwanted animals in shelters and therefore reduce euthanasia. Without awareness and knowledge we cannot make informed, wise, compassionate choices. Moreover, humane education is good for everyone: it teaches about the interconnected issues of human rights, animal protection, and environmental sustainability, all necessary components of a just and peaceful world for all. Shelters have an important role to play in education.

Choosing the Right Cat –
and What to do
When a Cat Chooses You

he biggest decision – and one many cat adopters do not consider – is making sure that you
adopt a cat that is right for you, your lifestyle
and your family. There are many things to consider, all of which
should be weighed carefully and honestly. Nothing is more
heartbreaking than seeing a cat being turned over or returned to
an animal shelter because it didn't fit in well with someone's life.
A cat is a complex feeling animal and deserves to be treated with
respect, and that mean being someone's well thought out choice.

There are many things to consider when adopting a cat, especially if it is your first cat. Age, breed, personality traits, background, whether the cat will be on its own or living with other
cats or pets, whether or not it has special needs, how much time

you have to devote to your cat, health, and what to do if you are the unexpected owner of a cat, are all things you must weigh out.

In addition, a potential cat owner must understand that a cat is *not* a low maintenance pet that needs little care. It doesn't require daily walks and to be taken outside to go to the bathroom as dogs do, but there is still a huge responsibility in owning a cat. Anyone who thinks that adopting a cat is an easier alternative to adopting a dog or that there is less responsibility should consider adopting another kind of pet, such as a goldfish, instead, or perhaps shouldn't adopt at all.

Kitten Cuteness or Cat Calmness

Everyone loves a baby, whether it's a human baby, a puppy, a kitten, or some other animal's youngster. Babies are innocent and appeal to our need to protect, nourish and comfort. But babies quickly become adults, especially in the animal world. A kitten is a cat in less than a year. What you will have to determine is

whether or not you want to go through that kitten stage along the way.

It is true that for many people, that wide-eyed kitten with its high pitched meow and need for reassurance is hard to resist. But kittens have a tremendous amount of energy and need constant supervision, which can be perfect for families with children but may not be for adults who might find the persistent demand for attention and its tendency to get underfoot somewhat irritating. It all depends on your lifestyle and personal choice. Do you mind having the curtains shredded or the couch clawed up while your kitten is still learning the rules? Do you have the time to devote to your kitten, since like human children, they demand and need constant attention and supervision?

If you do decide to adopt a kitten and you have a toddler or a very young child, make sure to oversee their time together. Kittens are more delicate than adult cats, and smaller kids do not always know how to carefully handle a tiny animal. A kitten can be a great lesson on how to treat animals gently. But you want to be within eyesight of your child and kitten, to prevent possible injuries.

Keep in mind that adopting a kitten is not the same as adopting a newborn baby. By the time you bring a kitten into your home, it has been weaned and is old enough to leave its mother. You could say that adopting a kitten is similar to adopting a 10-year-old child. By this age, it can run, jump, play and climb, but still needs constant supervision.

In addition, a kitten grows into a cat in a very short amount of time. That "cute" stage is over before you know it, and in less than a year you have a cat that in cat years is equivalent to being 15 to 20 years old. Of course, domestic animals never fully become adults the way wild animals do; their bodies merely age. No matter how old – kitten, mature cat, or senior – cats (and dogs) need us to care for them until the end of their days. In this way, your adult cat remains a kitten, just without the demanding personality, high energy levels, and mischievousness. And if you do have your own baby and think it will be amazing to have your child and kitten grow up together, it will not exactly go that way. By the time your infant is a toddler, your kitten is already a large, mature adult. Still, with an average lifespan of 15 to 20 years, your kitten-to-cat can provide your child with a lifetime of memories.

Having a kitten around *can* be a fun and wonderful experience. It can be heartwarming to witness a tiny ball of fur go from being adorable to maturely beautiful, and to know you are the only parent that kitten has ever known. But there is also a level of demand not experienced when owning an adult cat. As stated, kittens need constant attention and have little understanding of the rules. You will have to train your kitten to use the litter box, although this is something they tend to pick up quickly. Kittens also require more veterinary care in the forms of vaccines, booster shots, worming, and spaying or neutering – making that first year of ownership very expensive and time consuming. An adult cat, on the other hand, will not need the veterinary care required in the first year of a kitten's life and may also already be sterilized, saving you on those veterinary costs, although a senior cat may have health issues that can also be costly depending on what shape it is in when adopted.

In addition, when you adopt a kitten, you must kitten-proof your home, something not required when you adopt an adult cat. This means no dangling wires that could be chewed on or that could cause strangulation, no loose blind cords that can wrap around a kitten's neck and cause it to strangle, no access to deadly chemicals, cleaners and poisons (although, you should also take these precautions with an adult cat as well), and there's no need for constant awareness of where your kitten is and what it is up to at all times. This is not as difficult as it sounds, but it does demand more of your time than an adult cat who will enjoy playing with its toys but will also be perfectly happy to spend most of its day in your company or asleep on your couch or bed.

You will also need to train your kitten or it will try to run the show. Just like a child, kittens need to learn the rules and need to learn socialization. Kittens also represent the unknown. You don't really know who you are getting. With an adult cat, what you see is what you get. Your cat may become more comfortable as it settles into your home life and this can bring out its little quirks, likes and dislikes, but when you meet an adult feline, it is easy to see its personality and temperament, whether it is a quiet cat or more vocal, and whether it is sociable or more reserved. Not so, with kittens. A kitten's personality will change as it grows and its confidence level increases, so it is only later that you are able to determine whether or not the kitten is a good fit with you and your family.

When choosing to adopt a kitten versus a cat, be considerate of any other pets you have. A kitten's energy levels and playfulness might get on the adult pet's nerves. You will need to introduce the kitten slowly, to prevent them getting off on the wrong paw. Also, supervise their time together. A kitten is more delicate than an adult cat or dog, and can easily incur injuries. On the flip side, a kitten who has recently left its mother may find comfort in having another adult animal companion. Be patient. It may take several weeks or even months for your other cat or dog to welcome or at least come to terms with a new, attention-grabbing member of the family.

Finally, it should be pointed out that kittens have a much easier time getting adopted from shelters, although thousands are still euthanized each year from lack of homes. Adult cats have less of a chance at adoption and many never find a home. Everyone loves the kittens, even though adults make equally wonderful pets. When you adopt an adult cat, you are giving a wonderful animal a second chance at life and helping that cat beat the odds.

A senior cat has even less of a chance of ever finding a home. What you will get is a cat that may need a little more care and may be a little slower in getting around, but who will be forever grateful for the opportunity to be a member of your family.

Domestic or Moggie Versus Purebred or Pedigreed

Some people are under the misconception that a purebred or pedigreed cat is a better choice than a domestic, sometimes called *Moggie*, feline. The idea behind this way of thinking is that when you adopt a mixed breed cat, you do not know its background or what breeds it is mixed with and therefore are getting a less superior animal.

Nothing can be further than the truth and in fact, many purebred cats bring various health issues due to overbreeding or because certain traits and tendencies for certain diseases have become dominant over time. In addition, some pedigreed Oriental cat breeds, such as the Siamese, have unusual habits that are not completely understood, such as eating fabric. However, adopting a certain breed does bring with it certain personality traits and appearances not always evident in a domestic cat whose linage can only be guessed at. For example, if you prefer a vocal, intelligent cat, Siamese are known for their chattering and for being very bright. Or if you want a cat that looks like a wild cat, the Bombay has been bred to look like a black leopard (what some people mistakenly call a black panther).

In addition, some people prefer the cute pushed in face of a Persian. Other people want a cat with no tail, such as Manx, or the long hair of an Angora. Some people are simply hooked on a particular breed due to a wide array of traits such as hair length, body structure, ear shape, fur color or markings, or personality. There are 41 breeds that are recognized by the Cat Fanciers' Association, each unique in color, shape, size and personality. There is nothing wrong with adopting a specific breed, but make sure you do your homework.

First, only adopt from a reputable breeder rather than a kitten mill or backyard breeders. Reputable breeders know genetics and will not over breed, whereas it is not uncommon for non professional breeders to mate cats who are related. This can lead to genetic mutations, prevalence for disease, other health issues and even stillborn offspring. It can also ruin the purity of the breed. In addition, professional breeders do not adopt out just to anyone. Usually they have certain requirements and may require references and a background check.

The other difference in professional breeders versus kitten mills that churn out purebreds, often at the detriment of the mother cat's health, is that a reputable breeder is not in it for the money since the expenses incurred in providing the right care and environment to breed can override any revenue to be made. A good breeder simply loves the breed and the main motivation in being a breeder is to maintain the purity and survival of that breed, whereas backyard breeders are profit driven and that is the sole motivation for breeding.

Of course, be aware that when you adopt from a reputable breeder, you will pay the price. Adoption fees can run in the hundreds of dollars and the cat you adopt will not be sterilized, which can cost another hundred or so dollars if you do your part in not adding to the overpopulation problem.

Domestic cats or mixed breeds tend to be healthier because their gene pool is more diverse. Many purebred breeds are prone to certain health issues, which could be an additional cost. Plus, there is no limit to the amount of fur color and ticking, personality traits, variety in size, body structure and in hair length when you adopt a mixed breed cat. In addition, animal shelters are spilling over with domestic cats since the shortage of available homes is severely limited, which means when you adopt a Moggie, you are literally saving a life. Plus, you get a cat who is already sterilized (a requirement at almost all animal shelters) and who is up-to-date on its shots, all for a much more affordable price.

One thing to take into account if you have your heart set on adopting a specific breed: 20 percent of cats available for adoption at animal shelters are in fact purebreds. Many people find this statistic surprising, but keep in mind that breeders face the same challenge that shelters do – too many cats and not enough homes. In addition, purebred cats lose their homes for the same reasons domestic cats do: the owner dies and no one wants to take the cat, the owner moves and cannot, for one reason or another, bring the cat to the new location, someone in the family develops an allergy to the cat, the owner loses a job or economics for the surrender of the cat to a shelter, or for some reason the owners determine that the cat no longer their lives. Another way the purebred cats lose their homes is when owners allow their cats to wander free. All cats can get lost or picked up by animal control and wind up at a shelter. In any case, the only things you will be missing by adopting a purebred from a shelter are papers verifying its pedigree and the ability to breed that cat.

Choosing a Breed

There are valid arguments for adopting a purebred or pedigreed cat, as well as equally legitimate reasons for adopting a mixed breed or domestic cat. On the pro side of pedigree adoption is the argument that when you adopt a specific breed, you basically know what you are getting in terms of appearance and temperament, as well personality, but only to an extent since it can be argued that cats, like people, come with their own unique personalities. On the con side, however, is the fact that purebred cats tend to be less healthy than mixed breed felines because breeding to obtain certain traits tends to limit the gene pool and that results in an increase of health issues and potential defects linked to different breeds.

When it comes to purebred cats, there are also fewer choices of breeds than there are say dog breeds, for example. This is because dogs were originally bred to perform certain tasks that humans needed. In other words, dogs originally became our companions in order to assist of with labor. Cats, on the other hand, have been bred over time to be our companions and their breed-specific traits were and are simply a result of individual human preferences.

Ironically, 98 percent of cats are *not* purebreds, but there are 41 registered cat breeds in the United States that are recognized by the CFA, and 73 breeds recognized worldwide. According to the CFA, a cat is considered purebred if all of its ancestors are of the same breed, or if its ancestry includes cross breeding that has resulted in a new breed recognized by the CFA, such as the Bombay breed that has Burmese in its ancestral family tree. This ancestry, however, must be certified by the CFA or outside of the U.S. by the International Progressive Cat Breeders Alliance (IPCBA).

Exactly what constitutes a purebred cat has to do with consistency over time. In other words, cats who *breed true* in that they are able to consistently produce offspring who are the same as the parents with set traits in looks, size, color, hair length and to some extent personality. This is the result of selective breeding over many generations, and basically what this means is that what you see is what you get when two cats of the same breed are mated.

This purity of breed can go out the window if you purchase your purebred cat from a kitten mill or backyard breeder. Professional breeders will not breed their cats with other cats that are too closely related on the family tree or that do not meet stringent requirements of a particular breed. Their motivation, unlike the non professional breeder, is not for money, since, as mentioned, the expenses involved in care and veterinary services often outweigh the profit; rather, they are motivated by a love for the breed itself and the desire to keep that breed pure and continuous. In addition, a professional breeder will provide legitimate papers that include information about the cat's ancestry and parentage. This paperwork will include ancestors who were champion cats with registered names because serious cat breeders enter their cats in competitions, and those competitions have strict breed specific requirements.

If you decide to adopt a purebred cat and are not familiar with different breeds or aren't sure which breed you would like to share your home with, it is important to research the different traits linked to each breed. For example, Siamese cats are known to be "talkative" in that they constantly chatter. If you are someone who desires a more quiet type of cat, you might prefer adopting a Persian since this breed tends to be quiet and laid back. If you want a cat that does not require excessive grooming, then you should consider a short haired cat – or even one that is hairless like the Sphynx – rather than one with long hair, such as the Persian, that needs constant daily combing to prevent matting.

If you are attracted to a specific breed but couldn't care less about having certification paperwork validating its pedigree, then consider adopting a purebred from a shelter, where 20 percent of the animals there are purebreds, or from one of the many rescue groups whose mission is to save homeless purebreds from euthanasia. Check with your local animal shelter. Most keep a list of rescue groups on hand and are more than happy to provide contact information since these groups alleviate the dilemma facing all shelters – too many animals and not enough homes.

The mixed bag of mixed breeds

Cats that are not purebreds are called Moggies or Domestic cats or even mixed breeds, although the latter is somewhat misleading since the words mixed breed implies that there the cat is a mixture of two or more purebred cats and this is not always the case. Domestic felines tend to be healthier than purebred cats because of the wide hereditary gene pool that tends to breed out weak traits and keep the stronger traits.

But that does not mean that there aren't certain traits that Moggies or domestic felines, like their purebred cousins, can also carry or exhibit in terms of personality tied to color. For example, it isn't unusual for orange or ginger cats, 70 percent of whom are male, to be territorial, but they can also be unpredictable and feisty. Many tortoise-shell cats, all of which are female because the X chromosome determines the three colors, are considered loving but bitchy, whereas the tri-color calico, which is also always female, is often sweet and calm. Grey cats often seem standoffish and reserved but secretly love attention, and will show their wild side when playing a fun game of catch the string. Tabbies, often called tiger cats due to  the stripped pattern of their coats, are lovers of creature comforts and often are lap cats, wanting nothing more than a cozy place to sleep, a full tummy, and a friendly pet on the head. White cats are often laid back and shy, but also calm and loving. Black cats are often quirky and stubborn in their personalities but it's often a vie for attention since they are usually loving and friendly, whereas black and white or tuxedo cats tend to be very affectionate but independent. If ever there is a cat that tends to get lost, it's the tuxedo cat. In fact, black and white cats are the most common cats found at animal shelters.

Sadly, black cats have the least chances of adoption at animal shelters, probably due to their negative reputation as being unlucky or because people are more attracted to other colors, but their adoption rates go up around Halloween when they are often adopted to be used as a gimmick at parties or even tortured. This is why many shelters will not adopt out black cats during the month of October. Ironically, the tolerant, good nature of most black cats could have been their undoing during the witch hunts of the past since their friendliness and love of living indoors made them a favorite pet choice of the accused.

While color alone cannot determine a cat's total personality since this is also dependent on its upbringing and experiences, it may be something to consider when adopting your next cat. If you are looking for a cat that wants nothing more from life than to sleep curled up in your lap and are attracted to say a grey cat, you might want to reconsider and adopt a tabby cat instead. More importantly, however, is to meet the cat and see if you and the feline "connect" on a level that makes you realize that this is the cat for you. Cats, like people, are not stereotypes and coat colors and patterns are only one small measure to be taken into consideration when determining if a particular cat should be your next cat.

Feral cats: living life on the wild side

Feral cats are born in the wild, either by a mother feral cat or a cat that has kittens and then leaves them to survive on their own once they have been weaned. This is not to be mistaken for homeless cats who are abandoned by their owners or who are lost and therefore live on their own outside. The difference has to do with socialization.

Cats are not born with a desire to be our pets; rather, kittens are taught to be sociable by their mothers. If a mother cat is a feral cat – in other words a cat that was also born and raised outside without human contact – or if the mother has kittens outside and abandons them, then the kittens will rarely interact well with humans. A feral cat is, in fact, fearful and untrusting of humans, lives in the shadows, and will not allow a human to touch it. If the cat lives in a feral colony, this group of feral cats will also behave aggressively towards owned cats who are allowed to roam.

It is estimated that there are tens of millions of feral cats in the United States alone, and many communities attempt to control their populations through archaic means such as extermination and relocation. But increasingly, more humane methods of dealing with feral cat overpopulation are being used, such as the trap-and-release system or the trap-neuter-return procedure. This involves setting up humane traps that contain a can or bowl of cat food and work by enticing the cat into the cage, and once inside, the door to the cage locks behind it. The cat is then taken to a veterinarian who sterilizes it to prevent it from reproducing more feral cats. Once the feline has had and recovered from surgery and is given vaccinations to prevent the spread of diseases, it is released back into its feral colony.

That doesn't mean life for a feral cat is easy. Its life is often one of starvation, dealing with extreme weather changes, infections and attacks from other animals, and poisonings from humans. Feral cats must hunt for their food on a daily basis, which means they often go days without a meal. Feral cats are often ridden with parasites, and in many areas are picked up and euthanized by animal control agencies since they cannot be adopted out. But in some areas, there are organized feral colonies set up by the trap-and-release groups, where a designated caregiver feeds them and provides shelter and other medical needs. However, the average lifespan for a feral cat – or even an owned cat who is allowed to roam – is two years, compared to 14 to 20 years for a cat who lives entirely indoors.

Unfortunately, feral cats do not make good pets, which is why almost all animal shelters do not adopt them out. Adopting a feral cat is adopting an animal who will not be affectionate or sociable, may spray your home in an attempt to mark its territory, will probably not use the litter box, at least not consistently, will be mistrustful of your intentions, could even scratch you, your children or other pets, and will not be the companion animal most pet owners seek. Although feral cats live a difficult life, there is an order to their colonies, complete with a set hierarchy, and they are familiar with their territories. Life in the colony is complex, with various cats cooperating but also competing with each other for food and dominance. To put it simply, feral felines

have reverted to being wild and do not want to be someone's pet, and there are already not enough homes for the thousands of cats in animal shelters who are waiting for and wanting adoption.

The possible exception about feral cats not making good pets is if a feral kitten is rescued by its third or fourth week of life. The window of opportunity is small, but at this stage, a kitten is more trusting than an adult feral cat, and with proper and consistent handling can become socialized. The trick is, of course, catching a feral kitten without dealing with the aggression of its protective mother. By the ninth week, a feral kitten will remain wary of humans although kittens up to fourteen weeks of age can still be tamed, but the process is more difficult. After that age, the chances of socializing a feral cat is practically nil.

Stray cats that have gotten lost or are abandoned by their owners are another matter. Stray cats make great pets and actively seek to be someone's pet. You can tell the difference between a stray cat and a feral cat because a stray will often approach you and rub on your legs and purr, whereas a feral cat wants nothing to do with human interaction. But if a stray cat wanders up and invites itself in, it is important to make sure it is not owned before you decide to adopt it. You can either take the cat into your local shelter and ask to be contacted if no one claims the cat, or you can fill out a "lost report" at the various shelters in your community, put up "found" signs in your neighborhood, and place an ad in your local newspaper, while keeping the feline safe in your home. You can also take the cat to your veterinarian or community shelter and have it scanned to see if it is *microchipped*. Today, all dogs and cats who are adopted from shelters are chipped with a rice-sized microchip that contains the name, address and phone number of the owner. Pet owners can also have their own pets microchipped, which is highly recommended if your cat is an indoor/outdoor cat since thousands of cats who roam get lost each year, winding up at animal shelters where, after a period of time, they are either adopted out or euthanized. If, after making the effort to find the owner, no one claims the cat within a reasonable amount of time, then you can feel good in the knowledge that you are giving a home to an abandoned cat that wants and needs your companionship.

The Long and Short of It

Long- and shorthaired cats got their hair lengths the same way they got other traits – careful, selective breeding. Adopting a cat with long or short hair comes down to personal preferences. For those who prefer a purebred cat over a domestic one, the Persian is the most popular of the longhaired breeds. But with long hair comes extra work since longhaired cats need to be brushed on a daily basis. Otherwise, their hair becomes matted with tangles, debris and dirt, with the mats growing bigger and closer to the skin if left untangled, eventually actually pinching the skin of the cat. If a longhaired cat is not brushed daily, getting the tangles out can also be very painful.

In addition, longer hair can mean excessive shedding. If you have your heart set on a longhaired cat, then daily brushing can also lessen the cat hair shed around your home. Shorthaired cats need less brushing, but it is still important to occasionally brush its fur. A hairless cat, such as the Sphynx, does not need the grooming required of a longhaired, or even medium- and shorthaired, cat. But hairless cats have other challenges, such as special skin care requirements.

In addition to the Persian, other popular longhaired cat breeds include the Maine Coon, Norwegian Forest Cat, Somali, the longhaired Manx (formerly known as the Cymric), Selkirk Rex, Turkish Angora, Siberian Forest Cat, Javanese, Turkish Van, Himala-yan and the Balinese. There are also medium hair length cats, such as the Ragdoll and Birman. If you want a longhaired breed but don't want the work involved, the Ragamuffin is a great choice because its long hair rarely mats or tangles. Otherwise, there are plenty of shorthaired purebred cats to choose from – and many long-, medium- and shorthaired domestic cats to adopt.

The Silent Type Versus Chatty Catty

Cats don't meow to other cats. That form of communication is reserved for cat to human only. Some breeds are more vocal than others; some are the strong silent types. Siamese cats, for example, are extremely talkative and are known for the chattering sounds they make. They are also very active and enjoy carrying on "conversations" with their owners. Siamese demand attention and enjoy interacting with their people. If you like a home life that is quiet and want a feline who is laid back and nonintrusive, then a Siamese cat would not be the breed for you.

If you prefer a less vocal cat, then you might want to consider a Persian, Scottish Fold or American Curl. These cats tend to be aloof and reserved. The American Shorthair is another breed that is a quiet cat. The Oriental breed looks like the Siamese, but falls somewhere in between the constant Siamese chatterer and less talkative breeds. This breed is perfect for those owners who want some vocal interaction but not the demanding chattering of the Siamese.

Of course, when it comes to domestic cats, it is difficult to tell if they will be a chatty catty, a non talker, or somewhere in between, especially if you are adopting the cat as a kitten. If whether a cat is talkative or not is important to you, then try to spend time with the cat before adopting it. Many shelters have rooms you can take a potential adoptee into before you make your decision. Of course, many cats at shelters are afraid and confused, so it is not always easy to see a cat's full personality upon initial meeting. But there is always that cat that will put its paw through the cage bars if it is in that type of container and try to grab you or tap you as you walk by. If you take your time in picking out your cat, you can often get a feel for its personality and whether or not the cat will be more active and vocal than the cat in the cage next to it. Often an adoption decision comes down to whether or not you feel a connection with the cat you are considering.

Also, keep in mind that no cat – purebred or domestic – is totally silent. Cats need their meows in order to communicate with us. In fact, there are at least 19 different types of meows, differing in pitch, tone, volume and rhythm, and there are up to 30 different sounds that a cat is capable of making, including purring, squawking, screaming and trilling.

Loner Versus Lover

Like people, some cats are more sociable than others, while others are more solitary. Some cats thrive on interacting with their

people, while others enjoy the company of other cats or dogs, and still others do best being the only cat or pet in the home. Even if a cat lives with other cats or dogs, and even though all cats need personal space, some will prefer hanging out alone and will seek places in your home where it can get away from everyone else living there.

Unlike dogs, cats are not pack animals, but even the most solitary of cats needs some social interaction. In fact, a truly solitary cat is only solitary when there is not an assured food supply, such as in the case of some stray or feral cats. This is why owned cats who are allowed to roam sometimes bring their humans "presents" in the form of dead birds, mice or other smaller animals. It is a loving form of sharing. Even cats that live entirely indoors are known to bring toy mice or other stuffed animals to their owners.

It has been proposed by some in the past that cats are only affectionate with humans because humans provide food and other physical needs necessary for survival. But as any cat owner knows, cats can be quite affectionate, forming deep bonds with their humans and other pets in the home, and are known to go into a deep depression once that bond is broken or if an owner or another pet dies. Cats are not pack animals, but they do form partnerships based on love not on physical necessity. When some cats do not get attention from their humans, they will insert themselves into situations, such as insisting on sitting in your lap, sleeping with you, or sitting on your keyboard when you are trying to work on your computer.

If you desire a cat that is affectionate and wants affection, then a Persian is a great choice. Persians tend to be cuddly cats and will seek out your lap whenever it is available. Maine Coon, Exotic, Siamese, Ragdoll, Birman, Oriental, Sphynx, Burmese, Cornish Rex, Devon Rex, Tonkinese, Scottish Fold, Ocicats, Manx, Color-point Shorthair, Chartreux, American Curl, Japanese Bobtail, Turkish Angora, Siberian, Singapura, American Bobtail, Javenese, Turkish Van, Korat, Havana Brown, Ragamuffin, Bombay and LaPerm are also breeds that are known for their affection and need for interaction with their owners.

If you prefer a breed that is less demonstrative in its affections and more solitary, then you might want to consider an Abbysinian, Russian Blue or Egyptian Mau.

If you want a cat who falls somewhere in between – affectionate but not demanding of affection – then you may want to consider the American Shorthair, British Shorthair, Somali, Selkirk Rex, Norwegian Forest, Balinese or American Wirehair breeds.

Of course, it is a little more difficult to determine at first meeting whether a domestic cat is the loner type or a lover, compared to the reputation of a pedigree cat whose breed is known as affectionate or independent. And although color has been tied to personality, this is not a sure fail way either to ensure you get a cat who is openly affection or one who is more reserved in its desire for physical contact. Black cats are said to be independent but loving, but this display of affection is almost always on their terms. Black and white cats, also known as tuxedos, often love to butt heads (a form of a cat kiss) and enjoy a good petting. White cats tend to be more reserved, as are grey cats. Tabby cats are often demonstrative in their feelings, but orange cats can be unpredictable and even aggressive if they are not in the mood to be petted. Calicos can also be affectionate when the desire suits them, as can Tortoiseshells, although the latter is also known to reject any kind of interaction with their owners if they're not in the mood.

Again, try to spend time with a particular cat before making a decision on adoption. Personalities cannot always be determined by breed or color alone. Often it comes down to just clicking with a particular cat.

The cat you choose must also fit in well with your home situation. Some cats do well as part of a menagerie, while others prefer being the only cat. Black cats, for example, are said to better adjust to a multi-cat household than say more independent Tortoiseshell. However, cat color or breed alone cannot predict whether a cat will do well in a household with other cats, or whether it would be best suited as an only cat. Sometimes this has to do with your lifestyle. For example, if you have a job that demands long hours away from your home, you can prevent your cat from getting lonely by providing another cat housemate. Even if they aren't friends or in love with each other, it will bring them both comfort to know they are not alone while you're away. Just be prepared for an adjustment period if you are introducing a new cat to your resident cat. How to manage this is discussed later in Chapter 10.

Adopting the Special Needs Cat

Special needs cats can make wonderful pets, despite their medical conditions or handicaps. But adopting a special needs cat also involves dedication and commitment, and a willingness to go the extra mile.

A cat can be classified as a special needs feline if it needs medication to prevent its health from deteriorating or it is living with a chronic disease, or if it is missing a limb or eye, is blind, or if it has any kind of handicap that classifies it as disabled. Even senior felines are considered special needs pets because their chances of getting adopted are low.

Special needs cats are difficult to adopt out because potential adopters tend to view them as less of an animal or damaged or they don't want to invest their time in a cat that many only have a few years of life left. But the rewards of adopting special need felines are immeasurable. Many owners of these cats report that the cats seem to sense that someone has given them a new lease on life, and repay that second chance with an abundance of affection.

Blind cats and those with disabilities quickly adapt to their new homes. Cats are survivors by nature, and those with physical or visual problems will find ways to get around and compensate. The real challenge in adopting these special felines is that sometimes their care costs extra money. If a special needs cat needs medical care, then that is an extra expense. If they have been injured due to a physical mishap, such as being hit by a car, or from abuse, they may need extra medical attention or even surgery that may be costly. If they need to be on a special diet or develop a disease that requires surgery or ongoing visits to the veterinarian that also translates into extra money.

Senior felines may or may not need additional costly treatments, but they are often overlooked at shelters and rescue groups. The plus side of adopting a senior cat is that they are already trained and are more willing to learn your home's rules in order to fit in than a kitten or even younger cat. Senior felines are also more laid back than younger cats, and their personalities are already developed, so when you adopt them, you know right from the start what and who you are getting. Plus, even though there is the possibility that their care may cost more than a younger cat, you can feel good about the fact that your senior cat can at least enjoy its last years in a happy and safe environment.

Of course, you do need to be financially prepared. If your budget cannot afford the additional costs that may be involved in owning a senior cat, then you shouldn't adopt one. But the truth is, younger cats will one day be senior cats, so you should also be prepared for the medical costs they too will eventually need.

Adopting any special needs cat involves making a commitment to their requirements. It is not a decision that should be taken lightly since the last thing a special needs feline should have to face is another abandonment at a shelter. Ask yourself if you are prepared to face the additional financial commitments that are already in place or may arise in the future. You should also consider whether or not your living accommodations can provide the right environment that this cat may need. You will also need to make sure this cat will fit in with your other pets, children and other family members. If you aren't sure but think you want to give a home to a special needs kitty, then try fostering the one you want to adopt first to see if the cat is a good match. Lastly, ask your veterinarian what costs and other challenges may be involved in adopting a cat with special needs so that you are well prepared upfront.

If you believe that you can provide the right kind of loving home for a special needs cat, then check with your local shelter and also with special needs pet rescue groups in the area. You will not have a problem finding plenty of candidates waiting for the right home and for someone to give them a second chance at a happy life.

Choosing Your Healthy Cat and What to Look For

Unless your intention is to provide a home for a sick cat, then you want to make sure the cat you're adopting is in good health. That means being aware of certain clues that indicate wellness versus illness.

It may sound cold, but unless it is your goal to adopt a cat that is in poor health or needs someone to give it the best possible medical care, you should look over any potential cat you think you want to adopt with a critical eye. After all, giving a home to a cat is a long term investment – in time, money and emotions.

Pay attention to your first impressions, if you will. When you spot a cat you think you might want to adopt, are you filled with positive or negative feelings? Does the cat act alert or seem lethargic? Is it friendly, timid or aggressive? All of these can indicate underlying health problems.

Look for a cat with bright eyes as opposed to cloudy ones. Also pay attention if a cat's third eyelid, also known as a *nictitating membrane*, is partially covering the cat's eye or eyes. This third eyelid is pale pink and comes out from the inner corner of a cat's eye, partially covering the cat's eye or eyes when it is ill. It also protects a cat's eyes from injury. Check to make sure that there is no discharge coming out of the cat's eyes, ears or anus. Also, check the cat's nose. There should not be any discharge and the nose should be cool to the touch (although cat's noses do get warm from time to time) and slightly damp but not wet. If the cat sneezes a lot, that might also indicate upper respiratory disease or allergies.

In addition, you want to make sure the cat's teeth are in good or fairly good shape, and that its gums are not inflamed. Look to see if the cat is missing teeth. Feel the cat's body for lumps that could indicate cancer or other health problems. If you decide to adopt a kitten, make sure it has all 26 of its teeth. If it doesn't, then the kitten isn't old enough to adopt. Ideally, a kitten should be at least three months of age, but at the very least, it should not be younger than eight weeks old, since the first two months of a kitten's life is important to its development and is when the mother teaches it the necessary social skills it will need to make a good pet. Most shelters and breeders will not adopt a kitten out who is younger than eight weeks of age, but there are always unscrupulous breeders and pet shops that will.

Don't forget to look at a kitten or cat's fur when doing your health look over. A feline's fur should be shiny and clean. If the fur is dull or dirty, the cat may be ill since sick cats tend to neglect good grooming. Don't forget to check the fur for bald patches that could be indicative of ringworm, which is highly contagious to humans, or for fleas.

Finally, after you have adopted your shelter cat or a stray cat, it is a good idea to take it immediately to your veterinarian. Almost all shelters will test their felines for upper respiratory disease, feline AIDS and feline leukemia, and give them necessary vaccines such as rabies and distemper. But their budgets are limited and so is the exam that is given to pets who are adopted. Your veterinarian, on the other hand, can run a battery of tests that include blood work, stool and urine analysis, and testing for other potential ailments, and can do a thorough physical exam that includes checking for lung problems, skin irritations, lumps under the skin, or heart murmurs. This way, you can rest easy in knowing that there will not be any upfront health surprises, and if there are, you can then decide if this is a commitment you want to take on. But doing the once over when first meeting a cat of its eyes, ears, fur and temperament can prevent you from getting attached before you even get to the vet's office.

Sometimes the Cat Picks You

Sometimes a cat just shows up at your door and invites itself into your life. Other times, you might have your heart set on adopting a particular breed or a cat of a specific color, and wind up with a cat you never intended or dreamed you would be adopting. In other words, sometimes, despite your best intentions, the cat picks you.

If a stray cat has been hanging around, don't immediately assume that the cat is not owned or is unwanted. Cats get lost every day. Even inside-only cats escape and wind up lost. You only have to look in your local paper or on lost-and-found sites on the Internet to see ad after ad of cat owners desperate to find their missing cats.

Before you open your home to a cat that just shows up, make an effort to see if it already has a home. Place an ad in your local paper and online, and either take the cat to your local animal shelter or fill out a found report at your shelter. Also, ask the shelter if anyone has reported a cat matching the description of the feline you've found, and also place found posters around your neighborhood and at local veterinary offices and animal hospitals describing the cat and your contact information. If no one claims the cat after a few weeks, then you can feel comfortable about adopting it.

If you adopt a stray cat, immediately take it to your local veterinarian for a complete checkup, blood work, stool and urine samples, necessary vaccines, and spay or neuter surgery, if it is still intact. This is especially important if you already have cats, in order to make sure they do not pick up potentially fatal diseases.

If you find a cat you connect with at a shelter or pet store that is not exactly the cat you had in mind, try not to get hung up on what you had visualized to be your perfect cat and go with your feelings, provided of course that you can meet this particular cat's needs and possible expenses, especially if it is a special needs feline. Cats seem to psychically pick up on who is the perfect human for them, or as some say, who they want to own! Some of the best pets are those who choose us, rather than the other way around.

Meow is Just One Word – Understanding What Your Cat is Saying From Head to Tail

ommunicating with your cat creates a special bond between you. It begins by understanding the world from your cat's perspective. It also means understanding that a cat communicates in many ways – through sounds, body language, facial expressions, tail position, ear positions, grooming, scent, gift-giving, and whiskers.

Scientists who have studied feline communication note that cats have an elaborate and extensive vocabulary that includes hundreds of ways to tell humans what they want and need. In addition to the non-verbal ways a cat communicates, there are also numerous ways to say meow and there are many other sounds a cat emits, each having its own unique meaning.

In addition, cats are able to learn our words and commands and quickly pick up on non verbal clues as well. In fact, it is believed that cats can understand 20 or more human words, and are able to understand hand commands, voice tonal differences, and sign language. In addition, cats have been known to learn how to open doors, use and flush toilets, and do tricks on command, In fact, animal behaviorists claim that cats have an intelligence level similar to a two- to three-year-old child, and some insist it could be right up there with an eight-year-old child. To ignore that level of intelligence and not bothering to understand what you cat is trying to tell you is to miss out on developing a deep bond and a special relationship that is based on mutual understanding. And since your cat is more than willing to learn your language, return the favor and learn to speak "cat."

The Cat's Meow

Cats don't meow to other cats. It is a language skill they have picked up over thousands of years in order to converse solely with humans to have their needs met. In fact, vocalization is not a natural means of talking for cats since they prefer using a complex means of communicating that involves body language, scent, facial expressions and touch. But at some point in their relationships with humans, felines figured out that the non-vocal signals they give to each other do not work as well with humans, and so they developed a series of sounds as a means of communicating with us.

Understanding your cat's different meows is something easily acquired over time through careful observance and behavior. This will enhance the bond between you because cats are always learning our language and are always trying to figure out ways to improve the communications between them and us.

While each cat has its own unique sound or way of meowing, there does seem to be a universal way of meowing that is associated with different cat emotions. For example, if your cat does a short meow, this is a greeting or a way of saying hello to you. Multiple meows in a row mean that your cat has missed you and is happy or excited to see you are home. A meow with a higher pitch in the middle is your cat's way of asking you for something, such as food and treats or to be let outside. A drawn-out meow is a complaint, such as when time has passed the usual feeding time, whereas a low pitched meow is an attempt to invoke your sympathy because it is way passed the time of dinner, for example, and therefore your cat is sad. Cats who are depressed also make this low-pitched meow or yowl. A meow that sounds more like a scream or shriek occurs when you step on your cat's tail or almost close the door on its paw or some other painful mishap that is usually your fault.

A purr is that throaty vibrating sound a cat makes when it is contented and happy, such as when you are petting it. But cats also purr to comfort themselves, such as when a cat is at a shelter and is feeling lonely, when it is at the vet's and is scared, or when it isn't feeling well. Trilling is another interesting sound a cat makes. It is a high pitched sound that is a cross between a purr and a meow and is a sound of happiness and love, such as when you have been gone for a while and now you are home, or when a cat wakes up from a nap and searches you out, happy to find you. Mother cats often chirrup to their kittens as a way of finding them. A chirp sound is similar to a trill. A cat often chirps in anticipation of receiving a treat or meal, or something else it desires.

Some cats chatter. This is a sound made in response to spotting prey, such as when a cat sees birds or squirrels outside the window. Often, cats will mimic or make a chattering sound that sounds exactly like birds, as if your cat is trying to fool the birds into thinking that it is one of them. Cats also make an, "owww!" sound, which is repeated over and over as it carries its prey, such as a toy, around in its mouth.

A hiss is an angry sound a cat will make. It is letting you know that it will not tolerate whatever it is that is upsetting it. It is a serious warning. And while cats do not meow at other cats, only to humans, cats will purr when being groomed by another cat and they will hiss as a way to tell another cat or dog to back off. Cats can also growl. This is a low pitched sound a cat makes when it feels on the defensive or offensive in an attempt to appear threatening.

It is interesting to note that feral cats rarely meow or purr at humans, preferring to remain quiet and out of sight. They will, however, hiss when feeling threatened by people or other animals. In addition, pay attention if your cat is meowing incessantly; it could be a sign of a serious health issue or that your cat is in pain.

Body Posturing: Speaking and Understanding Your Cat's First Language

While it is true that some cats are more vocal than others – for example, Siamese cats are known for their nonstop chattering, while other cats barely make a sound – all cats use non verbal methods to communicate with us, other cats, dogs, and other animals. In fact, a cat's natural and preferred way of communicating is not through sounds at all – vocalization is reserved primarily for humans, since we tend to be one of the most vocal creatures in the animal kingdom and cats have clued into the fact that they can get a quicker response from us by vocalization rather than by body posturing.

Body language, on the other hand, is a cat's main language choice or first language if you will. To ignore the many signals and gestures a cat makes without taking the time to understand what each little nuance or posture means is to only partially have a conversation with your cat. And while there are dozens of ways a cat communicates via its body posturing, it is not that difficult to learn and is a language that can be mastered almost instinctively.

Some of your cat's body gestures will be unique to your personal relationship with it. Other body stances are universal among all cats. Here are some common body language posturing you can expect from your feline.

Tummy rollover

Many cats will stretch out and roll over, exposing their tummies as you walk by. Sometimes a cat will even reach out and tap you with one paw, as it rolls and exposes its stomach. This is a gesture of contentment, trust and relaxation since exposing your underside in the animal world is a vulnerable position. Just don't be surprised if your feline attacks your hand as you go to stroke its belly – many cats are very ticklish on their tummies!

Cats will also do the tummy rollover to other cats in your home. It is an invitation to play. And if you find your feline tummy up when napping, be happy – this is a supreme sign of trust and indicates that your cat feels safe and secure in your home setting.

Cat rub

Perhaps one of the best known feline gestures is the rub. It is the ultimate in cat compliments. When a cat rubs against your legs with its body, chin or cheek, it is marking you as its own. In other words, your cat really likes you and is laying claim to you. It is a sign of affection. Stray cats may also rub against your legs as if asking you to feed them or take them in, although sometimes you have to build up this trust. Feral cats, on the other hand, do not rub on humans. That is one way to tell the difference if a homeless cat just shows up.

When your cat rubs its cheek on you, it is releasing its scent or pheromones on you. Cats have five facial pheromones, in addition to their scent glands on their paws, pads, legs, perianal and base of the tail. Rubbing on you and you rubbing your hand on your cat's cheeks relaxes and calms your feline. Cats will also rub against your furniture, your walls, and other vertical surfaces and objects. This makes your feline feel secure because leaving its scent makes your home environment familiar to your cat. Your kitty might also rub against other cats or dogs in your home. This creates a group scent and can form deep and lasting bonds between them.

The best way to repay your feline for its show of affection is to rub it back. Cats love to be petted or scratched on their cheeks, under their chins, on the inside of their outer ears, or on the back of the head. Scratching the top of the base of the tail is another favorite spot for many cats and can actually cause them to go into a pleasurable trance.

Needing to knead you

Some people call it making biscuits, while others call it new-newing. But no matter what name you choose, when a cat kneads you as if it were kneading dough, it is a sign of happiness and deep affection. Kneading is what kittens do in order when nursing to get their mother's milk to flow. Apparently, it is a gesture they don't outgrow.

Most cats knead by alternating one paw and then the other while pushing into you. Some cats knead with their claws out, while others make biscuits with their claws retracted. Some felines use just the front paws, while others use all four. Some cats purr while kneading, others are silent. Because cats kneaded their mothers as kittens, they associate the act with comfort and protection. Take your cat's new-newing as a compliment and an indication that it trusts you as it would its own mother. And if the kneading hurts because your cat's nails are out while doing it, don't punish your kitty. It doesn't realize it is hurting you. Instead, keep your cat's nails trimmed and buy nail guards so that you both can enjoy this moment of affection.

The tale of the tail

A cat's tail can tell the whole story about its mood, feelings and intentions. If you want to know what is on a cat's mind or what its emotions are at any given moment, look at the tail.

For example, when a cat is feeling confident, it holds its tail up high. If your cat has its tail held high as it approaches you, this is another form of affection. Often this approach is followed by a rub against your leg. But if a cat has its tail held high but it is curled on the end, then the feline is not quite sure about you or whoever is approaching it. Also, if a cat has its tail held high but is flicking it, the cat is acknowledging that it sees or hears you, but is busy or is not interested in having any interaction at that time. This is not an insult – the cat is waving to you but something else has its attention.

When two cats approach each other with tails raised, they may sniff each other and sometimes rub their bodies against each other as they pass as if to cement the group scent and bond. But when one cat has a tail raised and the other does not, the first cat will often back away.

When a feline wraps its tail around a human's legs or curls its tail around another feline's tail, it is displaying friendliness. Tucked below or inside its legs, especially when combined with a low slinking walk, indicates anxiousness or insecurity.

If your cat feels threatened by a noise, another cat, dog or person, or for whatever reason, you will see its tail poof up like a bottle brush. If that is combined with an arched back and the hair along its back is on end, the cat is warning you to back off and to do it quickly.

A tail that is straight up and quivers could be a warning that a cat is about to spray, especially if it has not been spayed or neutered.

Even spayed or neutered cats will spray to mark territory if they feel that their territory is threatened or they are unhappy about a change in their environment.

When a cat thrashes its tail back and forth, it's a sign of aggravation, especially if the tail is moving back and forth in a quick manner. But some cats have what is known as a wagging tail, similar to a dog's wagging tail. It is a sign of a happy cat who likes to wag its tail. This is not the same as a cat who swishes its tail back and forth when it is unhappy. How you can tell the difference is by reading the rest of your cat's body language in combination with its tail movement and getting to know the little nuances of your cat that makes it unique.

If you want to try a neat trick with your cat's tail, say your cat's name when it is sitting or lying down and is relaxed. The tip of your feline's tail will flick back and forth every time you call it by name. This simple gesture is a sign that your cat knows its name.

Head to head

If your cat leans in and butts your head, take it as a compliment. Head bunting, also known as head butting or head bumping, is an affectionate gesture cats use to let us know that they love us.

Sometimes cats bump heads with people they do not know. If a cat butts its head on your head when you are meeting it for the first time or if your cat does it to someone you are introducing it to, take it as a stamp of approval. Cats are very sensitive creatures and seem to be able to tune into a person's feelings and character.

Head bunting is more than just a gesture, however. When your cat butts your head, it releases its pheromones or scent from the glands on its forehead on to you as a way of claiming you as its own. If a cat you are thinking of adopting does this to you, it has picked you as its new owner or is hoping that you choose it as your future cat. Head bunting, in other words, is a cat's way of bonding with you.

When a cat stretches its head towards you or another pet, it is telling you that it wants to be petted, or it is trying to see your face or the face of another cat or pet. When a feline is feeling aggressive, it may lower its head, although a submissive cat may also lower its head. How to tell the difference? Look at the cat's tail. Is it swishing back and forth or poofed out? Then it is in an aggressive mood. Is it hanging down between its legs? Then it is a submissive cat.

Your cat will also use its head as a way of ignoring you, either because it is upset with you or is just not interested at that given moment. Your cat will do this by keeping its head down and pulling its chin in, while turning sideways to avoid eye contact. Anyone who has owned a cat has gotten this partial back turning rejection.

One of the sweetest head gestures is the nose kiss. This is a nose bump where your cat will lean in and touch its wet nose to yours, then sniff your nose and mouth area. A feline has scent glands around its lips, so cats will do this as a friendly gesture and as a way of identifying you, a family member, or another cat or pet.

The Eyes Are a Mirror to a Cat's Soul

Kittens are born with their eyes closed and do not open them for seven to 20 days, so it is ironic that once open, a cat's eyes reveal a wide spectrum of emotions.

Perhaps one of the most endearing forms of eye communication is when your cat blinks a slow wink with both eyes at you or another cat or pet. This is known as "cat kissing" because this long blink is a sign of affection. In cat language, closing your eyes this way is a sign of trust. You will find that if you do the slow blink back to your cat, it may repeat the gesture. It is a loving moment of mutual trust between you.

The direct stare is another matter. People will often stare at a cat, but your cat might find this uncomfortable because staring is a threatening gesture to felines and a cat will avoid eye contact with another cat in order to avoid a confrontation. A cat who deliberately states at another cat, on the other hand, is being confrontational. The fight ends when one cat blinks or looks away. This might explain why cats will often pick out the one person in the room who is not looking in its direction and head in that person's direction. Often, this will be someone who does not particularly like cats, but who, by avoiding eye contact with the cat, has displayed a non threatening form of communication.

A cat's pupils can also be indicative of how it is feeling at any given moment. While it is true that a cat's pupils will expand in low light levels and contract in bright light, a feline also dilate its pupils when it is feeling under duress, over stimulated or frightened. By expanding its pupils, a cat can take in as much visual information as possible. On the other hand, when a cat is angry or aroused, it may narrow its pupils so that it is able to focus on whatever it is feeling threatened by. A cat will also contract its pupils when it is content, which is why it is important to access its entire body language, from nose to tail, in order to determine the emotional state your cat is in.

Your cat may squint its eyes when sniffing your smelly shoes or some other pungent odor. This is accompanied by your cat lifting its head, slightly opening its mouth, and curling back its lips. Cats have scent glands on the roof of their mouths that allow them to gathering information about a particular scent. On the other hand, your cat may display half closed eyes when sitting or lying down that indicates it is content, happy and relaxed. This is often accompanied by a still tail, ears forward and purring.

Getting an Earful

Cat ears have 32 ear muscles – the human ear only has six. In addition, cats can move their ears independently and can rotate them 180 degrees!

Pay attention to your cat's ears because they, along with its body and tail, tell the story of your feline's mood. If the ears are upright and point forward, then your cat is relaxed, inquisitive or happy. If the ears move sideways, then your cat is alert to certain sounds but isn't sure of what it is hearing. When your cat's ears go backwards or appear flat – also known as airplane ears – then your feline is irritable, angry, frightened, or is feeling aggressive. When your cat's ears swivel, it is paying attention to every sound around it, including sounds outside.

A cat's ears can also go backwards when it is curious, such as when it is also sniffing something and is trying to determine what it is. But when a cat is feeling anxious or irritated and its ears are back or sideways, this is usually in combination with other body language and vocalizations, such as the swishing of its tail or a poofed up tail, arched back, yowling sounds and hair on end. To truly understand your cat's moods or feelings, you have to pay attention to its body as a whole.

Watch the Whiskers

You can learn a lot about your cat's moods and emotions by paying attention to its whiskers. Whiskers that are spread or fanned out and forward facing indicate alertness, excitement and anticipation. The cheek muscles might be puffed out, which extends the whiskers past the muzzle. Your cats might also be fanned and pushed forward when your cat is playing or is intently "hunting" prey.

Whiskers that are straight and sideways mean that your cat is relaxed and content. This is also a friendly position of the whiskers, and it can also mean your cat is indifferent to whatever is going on around it.

Whiskers that are tightly spaced and are flattened back against the face are a sign of fear or timidity. Your cat does this to make its face appear smaller and non threatening. But your cat will also flatten its whiskers against its face when it is in an aggressive mood.

If your cat's whiskers are drooping down, it may be depressed or sad. Of course, these whisker indicators should be interpreted based on your cat's body language as a whole, in order to fully understand what your feline is saying and feeling.

Cat Smiles and Kitty Lips

Do cats smile? In the past, many animal behaviorists did not believe that cats actually grin, explaining it away as various muscle reflexes in the face that give the appearance of a smile. But that thinking is changing in that some animal experts now believe that cats and other animals might express happiness in the form of a smile.

Many cat owners swear that their felines do smile, and now they may have the experts in their corners in agreement with this line of thinking. Animals are more complex than originally thought, and feel many of the same wide range of emotions that we do.

Cats have bowed mouths, which can mimic a smile, so it may be difficult to say with absolute certainty whether or not a feline is actually smiling. But those who insist that cats do point out that felines also display an upside-down smile when they are unhappy.

Cats do grimace when it comes to smells. The expression is one where the feline's mouth is slightly open, the nose is slightly wrinkled, and the upper lip is drawn upward. It is an expression of disgust or displeasure at whatever the odor is that the cat finds distasteful.

Cats also express embarrassment. In this expression, the mouth is either closed or slightly open, and the lips are drawn backward, while the head swings slightly from side to side. Sometimes a feline will do this expression when it is rejecting another cat's friendly approach. It is as if the cat who is doing the rejection is nicely asking to be left alone.

Occasionally, you can catch your cat with its tongue sticking out. This may simply be due to its relaxed state of contentment, although it does look funny. When cats are anxious, on the other hand, they may lick their lips, although they also may do this when they are about to receive food or if they are about to vomit.

Yawning can indicate that your cat is tired, but it's also an expression of contentment and relaxation. Cats will also yawn when they wake up and stretch. Sometimes a cat will yawn in the face of a timid or anxious cat, as a way to help the other kitty to relax.

When cats are teased, embarrassed, have had enough of a situation, or are fearful or feeling aggressive, they often pull back their lips and hiss or bare their teeth – although it should be pointed out that cats rarely use their mouths to signal aggression. Rather, an open mouthed snarl or hiss is usually in reaction to feeling threatened and on the defensive, and baring its teeth is a way for a feline to take in all the scents that the aggressor may be giving off in order to better access the situation. Just as with a cat's other means of communicating, its mouth positions and reactions should always be interpreted in conjunction with its body language as a whole.

Licking Means Love

If you have never owned a cat before, it may puzzle you to be on the receiving end of your new cat's rough tongue as it licks your hand or arm, or to have your feline attempt to eat your hair. But these are natural habits when a cat loves and trusts its owner or another cat or pet. What your cat is doing is grooming you and since felines only do this to those they care about, it is a compliment of the highest order.

There are many reasons why a cat grooms, in addition to showing affection. Cats have a rough tongue that serves as a kind of comb, pulling out dead hair and parasites as the tongue rubs against a cat's skin. A cat's tongue is able to clean between its toes and up and under each nail. When a cat is done cleaning its fur, it then licks the fur to smooth out the hair, providing insulation from heat or cold. Grooming also distributes the oils of the hair evenly, which works as a sort of waterproofing moisturizer that makes its fur shine. Cats in fact spend about half of their waking hours grooming.

Grooming is a copy-cat activity that is learned in kittenhood. Mother cats lick their kittens, which in turn begin to groom themselves when they are about two weeks of age. When cats mutually groom each other, called *allogrooming*, they are expressing affection and cementing the bond they feel with one another. Interestingly, cats tend to groom or lick each other's heads and shoulders, two areas that are the hardest for them to clean on their own bodies. When your cat grooms you by licking you, tugging at and eating your hair, cleaning between your fingers, and accepting your petting in response, your cat is expressing its deep love and trust of you.

Grooming also has a calming affect when your cat is upset or fearful, or when it does something embarrassing or it is uncertain of how to react in an unfamiliar or uncomfortable situation. For example, if you stare at your cat or even if you do the slow blink and your cat blinks back, it might suddenly start grooming as a way to comfort itself. Or if your cat goes to leap on something and misses the mark, it might frantically groom itself as a way of calming itself down. Cats will also do this when confronted with a more aggressive cat – it might suddenly start licking itself in order to relieve tension.

When your cat grooms other cats in your home, they are exchanging their scents to form a group scent. And when your cat grooms you by licking, nibbling or gently biting, it is putting its scent on you and claiming you as its own. You might also find that your cat immediately grooms itself after you have petted it. In fact, what your feline is doing is comingling your scent with its own smell. On the other hand, when your cat has encountered an unpleasant experiences, such as being at the vet's and having the doctor touch it during the examination, then it may groom itself in order to wash away the scent of the ordeal and put its own smell back on its fur.

When your cat licks itself excessively to the point where it is losing hair or creates a bald spot, this might indicate that your feline is under stress or is allergic to the food it is eating or something else in your home or has an underlying health issue such as hyperthyroid disease. And if your kitty stops grooming or under grooms, this might suggest that your cat isn't feeling well or is depressed. In both of these cases, take your cat to the vet since this might mean your cat is under some kind of stress or needs medical care.

Also, remember to groom your cat, even though it may seem as if it doesn't need it since cats wash themselves. Try to brush your cat once a week – more often if it is a longhaired cat, in order to avoid matting which can be painful to pull out. Brushing your cat will feel good, get rid of excessive amounts of dead hair, thus preventing potential hairballs, and create an enjoyable experience for your cat. In addition, grooming your cat is the perfect time to look for any health issues, such as lumps or sores, fleas or unexplained weight loss.

Also, you should occasionally give your kitty a bath every few months or at least once or twice a year. Bathing a cat can be difficult and you may need to wear protective gloves, but it is important to do in order to remove the odor caused by your cat's saliva over time and to moisturize its skin and get rid of dead skin. Afterwards, don't be surprised if your kitty frantically grooms itself in order to dry its fur and redistribute its own scent. Your cat will just be doing what comes naturally.

Kitty Presents

Perhaps one of the most interesting ways that cats communicate their affection for their owners is by hunting and bringing prey – real or fake – to their owners. It could be a toy mouse, a stuffed animal, a ball or another toy, or it might be the real thing such as a captured dead mouse, a bug it has killed, or even a bird it has caught and killed, all to show its love for you.

You might recoil in horror when presented with some dead insect or animal, but your cat is showing off its hunting prowess, a feat that is never entirely bred out of the domestic cat, at the same time it is letting you know just how much it cares for you. Try to take this in the spirit it is given, and if the animal it has captured is still alive, you can always let it go – out of sight of your cat, of course!

Some animal behaviorists state that cats look at their human owners as poor hunters who need their help in hunting for the next meal. Others state that the wildness that still remains on a small level in domestic cats prompts them to hunt and share the bounty with their pride, that is, their family. Be sure to praise your cat for its present and its exceptional hunting skills.

The fact is, hunting comes naturally to cats, even though you feed yours a well balanced diet and it is well fed and maybe even overfed. This is why cats delight in games such as catch-the-feather on the end of a stick, chase-the-string, and chase-after-the-ball. Other activities favorited by felines are chasing the red laser light, and batting and catching toy mice. Some cats hoard treasured stuffed animals, while others have been known to fetch and bring back balls and crumpled up paper. And as any owner will tell you, stalking and attacking your ankles as you walk un-suspectingly by is another hunting game that cats find delight-ful. These games all involve hunting in one form or another, and when your cat catches the prize and brings it to you, it is wanting you to share in the fun.

Of course, hunting and bringing you dead animals is something you should try to discourage since some bird populations, for example, are often depleted by cats. The trick is thwarting this activity while not offending your cat by rejecting its present. The best way to do this is to keep your kitty indoors – a good idea anyway, as mentioned earlier in this book, since outdoor cats of-ten meet with unhappy fates. If your cat does go outside, you can prevent it from stalking live animals by attaching a bell to its col-lar so that any unsuspecting prey can hear it coming.

Getting your cat another cat friend can also keep its natural hunt-ing at bay. Instead of stalking any small creatures around or in your home, your cats will enjoy hunting and stalking each other – although your felines may still bring you gifts of toy mice and other non-living items since in your kitty's mind, you are the top cat and leader.

5

Teaching Your Cat to Speak Human

ust as it is important to understand what your cat's body language is saying and the meaning of the subtle nuances of different meows, it is equally important for your cat to understand what you are saying to it. Learning to communicate with your cat not only will make living together more enjoyable, it will deepen the emotional bonds between you.

It starts by simply talking to your cat, not just giving your cat commands. The more you talk to your cat, the quicker your cat will learn what you are saying, what the rules of the house are, and what the daily schedule of your home life is. In the process, you will also start to pick up on what your cat's various meows mean.

very intuitive when it comes to understanding the lan-
of humans. For example, if you use a high tone when
king to your cat, they will usually interpret this as friendli-
ss on your part, whereas a lower, stern tone suggests displea-
ure or even aggression. If you yell at your cat or are yelling in
an argument with another person – something you should not
do – you might notice that your cat's ears go back or flat and that
it seems upset. Cats are very sensitive to our emotions, which is
why they are able to successfully read our feelings and meanings,
and communicate their needs to us. Anyone who has owned a cat
will vouch for the fact that it doesn't matter so much what words
are spoken as to what tone those words are spoken in.

Having said that, many cat owners and animal behaviorists claim that cats are capable of learning what certain words mean – up to 20 to 35 words, in fact. Repetition is a huge part of teaching your cat your language, which is similar to how human adults repeat words to human babies in order to help them learn to speak and understand what is said to them, or how dog owners train their dogs, or even how a young child when placed in a home where a different language is spoken will eventually pick up that language. If you repeat words that your cat needs to know, such as "no," "come here," "treats," "sleep," "bed," "get down," and so on, you will find that in a short amount of time, your cat will associate different words with different activities or rules, and may even move towards the cat food, for example, if you say, "dinner" or "num nums" before you have even had the chance to open the bag or can. While a cat's natural language is non verbal, it will quickly learn verbal cues as a means of survival and as a way to fit in and get what it needs and wants from you and your family.

Name Calling, Verbal Commands, and Word Associations

When you are attempting to train your cat through words, be sure to be consistent in your tone, intention and expression. For example, you do not want to be telling your cat "no" while kissing it on its head or petting it, both pleasurable experiences for a feline. Otherwise, your cat will come to associate a behavior you do not want with the enjoyable action of being kissed or petted. Also, never, ever physically discipline your cat or yell at it. This could result in negative re-enforcement that leads to your cat acting out, such as going potty outside of the litter box, or it could frighten your cat, causing it not to trust you. Cats have a very long memory and once you lose their trust, it is very difficult to get it back.

If your cat is not behaving in the way you want it to, simply speak your commands in low, firm tones, which to cats translates to disapproval, and add a slight edge to your voice if you are trying to break or stop your kitty from behaving or acting in a certain way. Your cat will quickly understand that its behavior is not acceptable to you.

It is important to make the distinction between your cat actually understanding English (or whatever language its owner speaks), and understanding the results or actions of your commands. Cats learn by experience, so when they understand what you are saying, it has more to do with the actual event attached to the words rather than the actual words, although the sounds of those words will come to be associated with the experience. For example, if you are trying to break your cat's habit of jumping up on your kitchen counter, you might loudly clap your hands while saying, "Get down!" Cats do not like loud noises, so it will come to associate the loud clapping and the words, "Get down!" with being on the counter and will resist following this urge to jump up there.

Having said that, cats *are* capable of learning many words and commands, but the key to training your cat is to always follow your words with an action, such as the clapping of hands mentioned above. Raising the pitch of your voice is similar to how a mother cat communicates with her kittens, so saying the words, "Treats!" or "Din-din" in a higher tone can help your feline to associate those words with getting something good to eat.

A typical behavior of cats is to bother you right when you are try-ing to get something done. For example, when you need to work on something on your computer, but your cat wants to lie on the keyboard. This is the perfect time to say, "No!" or "Get!" in an authoritative voice and gently push your cat away. If, instead, you tell your cat, "No!" but pet it at the same time, you are just reinforcing its behavior.

As previously stated, a cat's natural mode of communication is non verbal, which is why it is important to combine words with physical action. Cats are quite capable of learning your com-mands, but it is always combined with the physical cues attached to them. If you let your feline go outside, standing by the door and saying, "Out" will eventually help it associate the word with the activity, or when you say, "Come on" or "Bed" and then walk in the direction that you want your cat to go, your cat will learn to follow you – provided that it wants to.

The exception to your cat linking an action with a word or command may be the first word that most cats learn, which is their name and not just their name, but any nicknames attached to it. A neat trick that you can try out is to say your cat's name and watch the tip of its tail flutter back and forth. When it stops, say your cat's nickname and it will repeat the tail fluttering. If your cat has more than one nickname, repeat each one and your cat's tail tip will again quiver back and forth. This means that your cat understands that each of those names is its name. Another example that you might want to try is to call your cat's name when you are in another part of the house than your kitty, and it will often come running in to where you are. The proof that your cat knows that this is its name and its name alone is that if you have more than one cat, each cat will only respond to its own name and not the names of your other cats.

In addition to learned commands or memorized names, simply speaking to your cat or having conversations with your kitty, even if it doesn't necessarily understand exactly what you are saying, can also reinforce the bond between you. For example, if you are flying and the cat carrier is beneath your seat, or you are riding in the car and your cat's carrier is in the seat next to you or behind you, or you are at the vet's office waiting while your cat is in its carrier, simply speaking softly to your feline while petting it through the bars with your fingers can reassure it and calm it down. It may not know exactly what you are saying, only that it is hearing your familiar voice and that your words are being said in a soothing tone.

This sympathetic understanding goes both ways, however, since cats also pick up on our moods. Many people report incidents when they are sad or crying, and their cats will sit close by or leap on to their laps as if to comfort them. The intuitive relationship between humans and cats and the ability for these two different species to communicate with each other is a beautiful and enriching experience.

Clickety Click

Words are not the only way to communicate with your cat to train it to understand what kind of behavior is appropriate or acceptable. Since felines associate commands with action, you might find that using a clicker is one way to easily teach your kitty the rules and have fun while doing it.

Clickers often work for training cats because cats sometimes make a clicking sound when tracking prey so it is a sound that they can relate to. Often clickers are used when teaching cats to do tricks, with a treat followed after they have performed, which is why it is a great tool to use to get your cat to stop doing certain actions and to reinforce good behavior.

A common misunderstanding about cats is that, unlike dogs, they cannot be trained. But the simple fact that your kitty comes running when you call its name or you call it to eat demonstrates that this is simply not the case. Another misnomer is that cats are not consistent in their behavior, that is, they may not jump on the counter while you are in the kitchen, for example, but they will jump up there once you have left. The real problem may in fact be inconsistency in your training of them or your communications with them.

If your goal is to communicate acceptable and unacceptable behavior for your cat, you need to first understand your kitty. Whereas a dog is a sociable creature who wants to do things to please you, your cat is independent and really doesn't care about praise or pleasing you, but it does care about food. It is also more difficult to motivate your feline, so combining clicking with a treat it really loves can make training easier – but you also need to have patience, and be consistent and creative.

Look at training your cat this way: it is a shared experience that can improve the communications between you and your cat, and deepen your emotional ties with each other. It requires spending time together, which also can only improve your relationship. And it can be fun, so it provides a mental and physical stimulation for your cat. Some of the training will, of course, be to change unacceptable behavior on the part of your cat, but some of it can be to teach it tricks, which will be an enjoyable experience for you both. This can include teaching your cat to fetch and retrieve a ball or some other item, but also useful behaviors such as sit, get down, stay, and come when its name is called.

You can either purchase a clicker at your local pet store or simply use a pen that makes a clicking sound. Whenever your cat does a behavior you approve of, comes when you call its name, or responds to a command, click the clicker and give your feline a tasty treat. Remember that cats learn through repetition, so you may have to run through the command a few times before your feline responds. Also, make sure you keep your training session brief, since cats have short attention spans and are easily bored.

In order to begin using the clicker as a means of communication with your cat, start by putting some favorite treats in a bowl and show it to your cat. Next, click the clicker and then give your cat a treat. Do this several times. Your kitty will associate the click sound with a reward. You will know that your cat has linked the click sound with a treat when you make the clicking sound and your feline automatically looks at the treats.

Next, decide which action you want to teach your cat to do first. Make it positive and save the negative behavior you want to break until after you have trained your cat to do a trick. For example, say you want to teach your feline how to sit. After it has learned to associate the clicking sound with a treat, wait until your kitty sits down on its hind quarters and then immediately click while saying, Sit, and then reward it with a treat. Soon, your cat will associate the word sit with something yummy to eat.

This type of communication through clicking stimulates your cat's brain. Always link a word with your cat's actions, reinforced by the clicker and then the treat once it has responded to your command, so that your cat will associate the word with the action. For example, if you want to train your cat to willingly go into its cat carrier – often a battle for most owners since the carrier often means the vet's office and riding in a car, two activities that can be stressful to a cat – click the clicker, say in (or whatever word you want to link to the carrier), put your cat into the carrier and then give your cat a treat. You might want to have the treat waiting inside the carrier so that your cat will enter it willingly in order to retrieve it. Once it has entered, click and then say, "In!" After repeating this, your cat will associate the carrier with the pleasant reward of a treat, rather than with the negative connection to the vet's office or a ride in your car.

Using a clicker is also a great way to break bad habits. If your cat has the habit of climbing up on something you don't want it to get on, simply click the clicker, firmly say, "No!" or "Get down!" and then have a treat waiting for it when it jumps down. Clickers are much better than using punishment, which almost never works and only serves to create stress and distrust between you and your cat. In addition, stress leads to acting out, like eliminating outside of the litter box, creating another stressful situation.

Try to use the clicker often, whether it is to reinforce a good behavior or break a bad one, and make sure you always follow up the click with a treat. This includes situations such as when two cats in the family are hissing and acting aggressively towards each other. You can cut the tension with a simple click that will catch their attention since they will know this means treat time. Use it when your cat goes to scratch on your furniture instead of the scratching post. Then take your kitty over to the post, move its paws to scratch it, click again and give a treat.

Bad behavior is often the result of either boredom or inconsistent training. Using a clicker sends a strong message to your cat about what is and is not acceptable, and reinforces the positive rather than the negative. In addition, clicker training strengthens the connection and affection between you and your cat, alleviates stress, and is a great way to get you and your cat talking.

Cat Sign Language

Using sign language is a great way to train and communicate with your cat because a feline's first language is non verbal signals that cats give to each other and to humans. Using sign language or hand gestures does not have to be the complex signing of the American Sign Language (ASL), although that certainly will work and is sometimes used by deaf people who sign to their pets who in turn understand perfectly what their owners are saying. If you do not know ASL or want to use a simpler method, you can use whatever hand commands you devise and your cat will easily learn and adapt to this form of communication, provided that you are consistent. Cats, it should be noted, have excellent memories, and once a lesson is learned, it is usually retained for life.

Combining these hand signals with words is a great way to reinforce this way of communicating. For instance, if you want your cat to sit in your lap or come up on your bed with you, you can pat your lap, the seat next to you, or your bed and say, "Up!" Or if your cat is on the kitchen counter, you can say, "Down!" in a stern voice with an unhappy face and use your finger to point down towards the floor. If you want your cat to come to you, say, "Come here!" in a high pitched voice and beckon with your hand. Some other easy hand gestures include using an open palm facing out to your cat to indicate when you want it to stop a certain behavior, pointing your index finger to your cat's nose (without touching it) while making strong eye contact when you want to communicate the word, "No," or pointing to your feline's food bowl and then pointing back at your cat if it is time for your cat to eat, while saying, "Din-din" or whatever word you use for a particular mealtime.

Sign language and hand gestures are especially helpful if you have a hearing loss or have adopted a cat who is deaf. White cats with blue eyes have a high rate of deafness due to a genetic mutation, but any cat can suffer from a hearing loss, particularly as it ages. Since cats use body languages as their primary way of communicating, a deaf cat makes a perfectly good pet since it will quickly adapt and learn whatever hand signals you teach it.

Cats sometimes have their own way of using sign language to communicate to their owners. Many cats will often use their paws as a way to signal what they want. Some cats will tap their owners on their arm when they want to be petted or fed. Cats have a fantastic inner clock that tells them that it is the time of day for their daily activities, especially for when they are normally fed, so tapping their owners at meal time is as if they are saying, "Hey, it's time for dinner!" Cats have also been known to tap their owners' hands with their paw as a way to demand petting, and many cat owners also know that familiar tap on the face that some felines give their owners if they have overslept past their cat's breakfast time. Take advantage of this natural way of communicating to respond to your cat's paw gestures with your own hand signals.

Remember to be consistent and patient since it may take some repetition before your cat catches on to the meaning of your hand gestures. Keep in mind that cats are very sensitive to and observant of our body language, which makes sign language a natural extension of that. But if you stick to it, you might discover that signing to your cat is a more successful way of communicating that simply stating words or commands. Regardless of whether you teach your cat ASL or devise your own hand gestures, teaching your feline sign language is mentally stimulating for your cat and a great way to form an intellectual and emotional attachment between you.

Communicating Through Grooming and Petting

Grooming your cat is not a verbal language in the sense that teaching your cat words, commands or hand signals is, but it does speak to your feline on a deeper, intuitive level, beyond just sprucing your cat up. Grooming, in fact, can be a shared personal exercise that can gain your cat's trust and communicate the mutual affection between you.

When two cats groom each other, this indicates a form of friendship. In addition, cats will only groom another cat in the areas of the body that the other cat cannot reach – such as the top of the head, cheeks, ears and back of the neck. When you pet your cat in these areas, you are displaying a form of grooming to your feline as if you were cleaning it, and your cat finds the task to be physically and emotionally pleasing. You are, in fact, communicating your love for your cat.

We do not have the rough tongue or other cat means to actually groom our felines the way they do each other. But brushing your cat is a close second and most cats enjoy the experience. Of course, when you do this grooming is equally as important as doing it. Try to schedule your cat's grooming session for when it is in a relaxed state, such as after it has eaten and is ready to take a cat nap. Your feline won't want to stop and be groomed when it is on the move or ready to play. Also, make sure you are feeling at ease and relaxed when you go to brush your cat since cats can instinctively pick up on any negative emotions or stress.

Also, keep the time you groom your kitty to about ten to 15 minutes, since cats have short attention spans. If your cat is the type that doesn't like to be held, sit it down on the ground or couch and position yourself next to it, rather than trying to groom it in your lap. Start by brushing or combing your cat's head and cheeks, gradually moving down its back towards its tail. After your cat gets used to you grooming it, you can try to brush its belly, if it will let you without it turning into a free-for-all of biting and scratching, since this is usually a very ticklish or sensitive area of the body for most cats. Eventually, your kitty might also let you touch its feet, which is important in order to get it used to those times when you will need to clip its nails.

Bathing your cat is another form of grooming that is a little trickier since most felines do not enjoy getting wet or getting in water and will not interpret this as a loving form of communication. However, bathing is necessary in order to keep your cat smelling clean and so that its skin does not get dry and flakey, but you might need to get someone to help you perform this task. In any case, be sure to give your cat lots of praise and a treat when it is over.

What your cat will probably enjoy after the bathing fact, however, is the brushing you should perform to smooth out its hair – and it will be happy with how its skin will feel once this dreaded task of getting wet and shampooed is over. It is very important to use shampoo made especially for cats, however, since human shampoos can be toxic to cats!

Grooming your cat should be done on a weekly basis – more often if your cat has long hair, to prevent it from tangling and matting. Make it a special you-and-me time with your feline and eventually your cat will see this session as an enjoyable opportunity to bond with you. If you have more than one cat, you might want to get each one its own special brush or comb that smells like them, although sharing scents via a communal brush can also be viewed as a form of allogrooming.

Also, remember that when you pet your cat, scratching its cheeks, around its ears and under its chin, you are also mimicking the way cats affectionately rub on each other. Petting is something that can be done at any given time or place and takes no effort. It is a form of communication whose importance cannot be stressed enough. It tells your cat that you love it and is a form of allogrooming that spreads your scent on to your cat and its scent on to you. Plus, it is a rare cat who doesn't love to be petted as evidenced by the fact that many cats seek out their owners petting.

So when you are walking past your cat or sitting in your favorite chair watching TV, reach down and rub your cat. Even if the act only lasts for a second or two, it is a way to acknowledge your cat's presence and communicates how much you value your feline's company. And when your cat in turn grooms you by licking you or eating your hair, it is telling you that the feeling is mutual.

Play Ball

Playing ball – or playing any kind of game – with your cat satisfies its need for attention, vents its drive to stalk prey, and enables it to use up excess energy. Plus, it is fun and cats are all about having a good time. Partaking in games that your feline enjoys provides intellectual stimulation for your cat and speaks to its hunting instincts. It is yet another enjoyable opportunity to improve the communications between you and your feline, and therefore, enhance your relationship.

Cats love balls. They fulfill a feline's enjoyment of batting things around, and when batted, balls bounce. Many cats will bring a ball back to you, similar to the way dogs chase and fetch, wanting you to bounce or throw it again. If your cat captures a ball you have thrown and brings it back, reward your kitty with a treat. This will reinforce the chase and fetch behavior. Cats also like to play a form of soccer, so flick the ball with your finger and your cat will more than likely chase after it, hitting it with its front paw to make it go further. Be sure to stock up on plenty of balls, since they tend to get lost under the couch.

One fun game to do with your cat is to play dead. Lay on the floor and act like your dead. Your cat won't be able to resist the temptation to come over to sniff you. When you feel your cat's breath on your skin, leap up and chase your cat. Another great way to appeal to your cat's love of stalking and pouncing is to play hide-and-go-seek. Hide behind a wall near where your cat is and peek out. Make eye contact with your kitty and then pull back. Your cat's natural curiosity will get the better of it and it will have to come see what you are up to. As it nears the wall you are hiding behind, hide around another corner. Your cat will continue to seek you out. At some point, jump out and then run. Your cat might chase after you in a form of cat tag.

Of course, some of the most favorite games of cats are pole games, such as a feather or bird on the end of the stick that your cat can bat, or you pulling a string tied to a pole and your cat chasing it. A red laser light that can be stalked and chased is also a popular cat game. In addition, cats love to pounce on and bat around toy mice, and some felines even like to carry around these mice or small stuffed animals that they may then bring to you as "presents." When cats live on the streets, they are forced to chase and catch small animals and insects in order to eat, so these games appeal to your kitty's natural need to stalk and catch small creatures. However, it does not take long for a cat to become bored with a toy. Keep a lot of different types of toys on hand and rotate them and the games you play with your cat often. Also, put your cat's toys away between games so that when you get them out, it will signal to your kitty that it is time to have some fun with you.

Also remember that cats that are bored often display destructive behavior, such as clawing up furniture and eliminating outside of the litter box. You can break those bad habits by spending more time playing with your cat because play is a great behavior modification tool. Instead of communicating displeasure at your cat's negative activities, you will be redirecting your cat's focus on something positive – play – and at the same time letting your kitty know that you enjoy interacting with it. As a result, your cat will more than likely stop whatever bad behavior it was displaying because playing with you makes it feel happy, wanted and noticed.

Playing games is also a great way to win over a new cat in your home and form a positive bond between you immediately. Communicating through play with a new cat sets up a sense of immediate trust. If you have an older cat that is slowing down and doesn't seem interested in games that require a lot of physical activity, then get it a food ball. It will keep your senior kitty mentally stimulated and active, while it rolls the ball around in an attempt to get the ball to dole out its treats.

Cats are physical animals who communicate through physical actions, so enriching their lives through games with them appeals to their social personality and natural way of interacting. It doesn't take much of your time to engage your cat in play, since cats have short attention spans, but by spending just a few minutes a day, the payoff will be a happier, more loving feline and a closer relationship between you two.

Tricking your cat

In addition to playing games, you can also improve the communications between you and your cat by having it learn to do tricks. This *is* a form of play that mentally stimulates your cat's love of learning. And since it is an activity that must be done together, it is also another avenue for you to both spend more time together.

You will have the most success in teaching your cats to perform tricks if you use positive re-enforcement, such as praise and treats. You will also need to have a lot of patience and use a lot of repetition since it can take a while for your cat to catch on and remember the trick. Cats can be a taught to sit, lie down, and even jump through hoops. Some cats have been able to learn how to open doors by turning the door knob, while others can be taught to open drawers. Since word association and hand signals are often learned when teaching cats to do tricks, this is another way to enhance your cat's communications skills.

Cats are able to learn tricks because they have sophisticated brains that are very similar to humans. This brain is able to connect the dots between being asked to perform a trick, performing the trick, and then getting a reward for doing the trick. Be sure to keep plenty of treats on hand when teaching your cat tricks, since cats are motivated by food.

As mentioned earlier in this chapter, clickers are great devices for teaching your cat new things. Just as you can train your cat certain words and commands by using a clicker, you can also use this device to teach your cat tricks. You can also use a pen or anything that uses a clicking sound. Associate a word for each trick, say the word and then click. The clicking sound will alert your cat that it will receive a treat upon performing that trick.

When training your cat to do a trick, make it a short session of about five minutes. Cats have short attention spans and will lose interest if you make the time frame too long. It is also a good idea to do your training when your cat is hungry, so that it will be more motivated to do the trick in order to receive a treat.

If you have more than one cat, separate them so that you are teaching a trick one-on-one. If you have your other cats in the room, they may distract the cat you are trying to train. Make sure the room you are teaching the trick in is also quiet and free of distractions.

Next, sit on the floor so that you are at eye level with your cat. This way, you can respond immediately with your clicker, praise and treat. Start by tossing a treat and clicking. After doing this a few times, your cat will understand that after the click comes the treat. Also, only use the clicker for when you are teaching your cat a trick (or for when you are doing behavioral training, as mentioned earlier in this chapter) so that it will associate the click with performing and receiving a treat.

After you have used the clicker and given a treat several times, next throw the treat a little further, so that your cat will have to work harder to get it. This gets your feline used to having to do something to get the treat.

If your trick is to teach your cat to sit on cue, then take a treat, let your cat smell it, and then raise the treat over your kitty's head. As your cat raises its head and its eyes follow the treat, it will automatically sit down. When it does, click the clicker as you say "sit," and then give your cat the treat. After a while, your cat will associate the word, "sit" with the clicker and best of all, the treat. If your goal is to teach your cat to jump up for a treat, then hold your arm and hand out at chest level with a treat between your thumb and fingers, click as you say, "jump!" If your cat is motivated by the treat, it will eventually leap up to receive it. There are many tricks you can teach your cat, including giving you a high five, laying down, rolling over, turning in a circle and come, for example; but make sure you only teach your cat one at a time to avoid mental overload and confusion. Once your cat has learned one trick, then you can move on to a new one.

Also, make sure that the words you choose to associate each trick are ones not used for anything else. You want your cat to link each word to a specific trick. In addition, do not reward your cat simply for sitting down or doing another trick when you have not directed it to do so. Only give it a treat when you have asked it to perform a trick. You want your cat to be able to perform on target, when you say the word attached to that trick and then click. Otherwise, your cat will not link the verbal association with the trick.

One reason why using a clicker to train a cat to do a trick is so successful and makes it easier to train your cat is that your feline is used to your voice and hears it all the time, sometimes even tuning you out. The clicker, therefore, becomes a unique form of communication associated with a specific trick. Plus, your cat will come to know that the clicker and the subsequent performance of the trick equals something good to eat.

You can also teach your cat to do tricks by using sign language and hand signals or even clapping. But clickers have been found to be highly successful tools, perhaps because the noise is not loud or threatening and easily grabs your cat's attention.

Also, make sure that the treats you choose as rewards are different than your usual treats. Pick really good treats that you know your cat loves. By making them a different treat than your cat's everyday ones will be motivating and exciting for your cat. Once your cat has mastered one trick, move on to a new one, but as stated, only teach your cat one at a time. Felines are highly intelligent and are easily trainable, and teaching them tricks relieves them of boredom, but they must have the right motivation. For dogs, that motivation is pleasing you; for cats, it is the reward. Training your cat to do tricks is another great way to spend one-on-one time with your kitty, keep it mentally stimulate, provide fun and exercise, and expand the perimeters of your human to cat communication.

Learning to Speak Meow

Just as we can train cats, they also are able to train us by teaching us the meanings of their various meows and body language. As stated in Chapter 4, cats reserve meowing for humans, rarely using this form of communication with each other, with the exception of hissing and screaming. This is because humans tend to be unobservant and often clueless when it comes to non verbal communication, so cats have evolved to understand that meowing is the only way they can get our attention. This is because while felines are able to take in their whole surroundings at once, people are prone to concentrate on one or two things at a time, such as reading a book while watching TV. However, we will shift our focus when interrupted, and cats have caught on to this – which is why they have evolved to use a variety of meows in order to grab our attention.

This is no simple feat. People often compare cats to dogs, the latter able to learn around 100 words or commands, versus a feline's ability to learn 25 to 35. But while dogs can understand more words than cats, they can only vocalize about 15 sounds, whereas cats can make up to 100 different vocalizations, and each of those meows is unique to each cat. Dogs may be better listeners and more willing to be trained due to their pack mentality, but cats make more of an effort when it comes to actually speaking to us.

In addition, many cats have learned that if they meow while near certain locations where they want action, such as when you are in the kitchen with your cat and it meows next to the cabinet door where the cat food is kept, or if they come into a room where you are, and then meow and exit that room, continuing their meowing as they walk away, they are likely to get exactly what they are asking for. Cats know that by not letting up on their meows, we will probably get up to take care of their needs, if for no other reason than to get them to stop. In other words, we can train cats through our words and actions, but they are also able to train us through theirs.

Your cat's different sounds mean different things, and over time many cat owners come to find that they know exactly what their cats are saying. It is, however, just as important to learn to speak your cat's language as it is for it to learn yours if you hope to have a close relationship with your cat.

This goes beyond just understanding the variances in your cat's meows. It means talking back to your cat by mimicking your cat's body language, kissing your cat with your eyes, or touching your nose up to your cat for a nose kiss, and even meowing at your cat. It means understanding that petting your cat is a form of communication with it, and allowing your cat to pet you in return in the form of licking and rubbing against you.

Speaking meow also means changing your tonal pitch when you are speaking to your cat, as described in Chapter 4. Higher pitches equate to happiness and love for your cat, just as lower, firmer sounds indicate displeasure or a command. You can even take this further by hissing or making a spitting sound when your cat isn't behaving or is doing something you don't approve of.

If you have a cat that is the silent type or who does not meow much, speaking with it can get it to come out of its meow shell, so to speak. Getting your cat to talk more will improve your relationship and the communication between you.

This involves talking to your cat more and using its name in every conversation. If you want your cat to understand your human words, then speaking human to it is very important. Think of it in the terms of how people speak to babies so that over time the baby comes to understand human language. Talking with your cat is mentally stimulating for your cat because felines will work at trying to understand what it is you are trying to say.

For example, when you get up in the morning, greet your cat. When you are in the kitchen preparing a meal and your cat is lying nearby, have a conversation with it. Ask your cat wants a treat or go over and tell your kitty you love it, and then kiss it on its head. Say goodnight to your feline when you go to bed. Talk as much as you can with your cat and do it every day. Thread its name into the discussion as often as possible.

This tells your cat that you are interested and that you care. Over time, not only will you start to understand the subtle nuances of each meow, but your cat will also begin to understand what you are saying. You will know you have succeeded when you say something about your cat to another person and your cat reacts by doing the very thing you told the other person about!

If your cat is the silent type and starts to meow more, take time to listen to it. You may not understand what your kitty is saying at first, but over time you will discover that you do. By speaking cat to your cat, it will deepen its affection for you and create an environment that is more stimulating and interesting for your cat.

What Your Cat Doesn't Say Could Harm It

hen it comes to your cat communicating its unhappiness, displeasure, depression or illness, it is easy to miss the signals. Cats often hide their illnesses or sadness in an attempt to hide their vulnerability. While it is true that an unhappy cat or one that feels threatened may hiss, spit or howl, this is often just a preliminary warning of a more serious problem. It is important not to take any unusual behavior or actions at face value, but to dig deeper, be more aware, and look for warning signs that your cat has a bigger problem – one that can seriously affect its health.

Outside the Box

If your cat suddenly starts to eliminate outside of its litter box, it's time for you to think outside the box. Before you jump to any conclusions, make sure you are keeping the litter box clean. Cats, like people, vary in what they can put up with. Some felines can let the pee or poop pile up in the box before they decide they have had enough. Some will rebel if you go more than a day or two before scooping. And some are so fastidious that they will eliminate outside the box if it is not cleaned the second they have peed or pooped in it. Only you know your cat, so take your cues from it and clean accordingly. Ask yourself: would you want to use the toilet after someone who has forgotten to flush? Chances are, you wouldn't and neither would your cat.

If litter box cleanliness isn't an issue, then the next thing you should do is try to view the box from your cat's perspective. Is it located in an area of heavy traffic? If so, move it to a more private location. Cats are picky about their privacy and they do not like to be watched when they are going to the bathroom. Is another cat in your home bothering the cat while it is trying to go potty? If so, then keep an eye on the situation and shoo the other cat away when kitty needs to go. Is the litter box difficult to get to? If so, then again, move it to a more convenient but private location. Is your cat getting up in years and the litter box has high sides that are difficult for your senior cat to maneuver? If so, then replace it with a litter box that has lower sides. Or if your cat is a large sized kitty, make sure that the box gives it plenty of room to move around in the box. If you have recently changed litter, your cat might be telling you it doesn't like the new brand – especially if you have switched to a scented kind, since perfume can sometimes smell like cat pee to a cat. Also, consider replacing the box if you have had it a while. Plastic tends to hold in odors and perhaps it now smells of cat urine you cannot detect, but your cat's heightened sense of smell can.

If none of these situations is the problem and your cat isn't under stress due to a move or a new member of the family or a new pet, then it is most likely a health issue. In fact, in most cases where a cat eliminates outside the box, there is a medical reason for it. Take your cat to your veterinarian for a complete checkup, since many illnesses and medical issues require immediate attention. The reason for the elimination outside the box might be due to a minor health issue, but it is better to find out for sure. Your kitty's life could pay the price if you choose to ignore the problem.

Constipation

Constipation is a common ailment among cats, particularly with male or older kitties. It also can lead to litter box issues. You might hear your cat crying or yowling in pain when it is trying to go inside the litter box, and when it finally can go, it eliminates outside the box because it comes to associate the litter box with pain. Another sign that your cat is constipated is if it is straining to go with little or no success. Take your cat to the vet immediately because constipation can be life threatening.

There are a number of reasons why your cat may be constipated. It might have an intestinal blockage from a hairball or a foreign object it has eaten that makes it difficult for feces to pass through the intestines. Or a tumor might be causing the obstruction, making it tough to eliminate. Your cat might also be dehydrated, resulting in either small or hard feces, or not defecating for days.

Constipation can also be caused by obesity. Not eating enough fiber or eating only dry food can also cause your cat to be constipated. Fiber moves the feces through the intestines, and dry food can eliminate moisture that also moves the feces along. Lack of exercise is also a cause of constipation in cats, as can arthritis that makes it difficult for your cat to squat and go.

Constipation can also be a result of feline diabetes or hyperthyroid disease, which is why you want to make sure that your veterinarian does a thorough checkup for any underlying health issues that can be life threatening conditions. Your vet can also prescribe medications or remedies to help your cat go, since if constipation is left untreated it can lead to *obstipation*, which is the inability of a cat being able to empty its colon. If a cat cannot empty its colon, it becomes packed with large amounts of feces and can lead to a condition called *megacolon*, which is when the large intestine and colon become enlarged and filled with hard fecal matter and is unable to contract effectively in order to evacuate the stool. This can lead to unproductive straining, lethargy, appetite loss and vomiting – with surgery being the only solution.

You can help prevent constipation – as well as elimination outside the litter box – by making sure that your cat eats wet canned food that adds moisture to your cat's diet, and that its dry food is high quality with plenty of fiber and no fillers. Also, see to it that your cat gets plenty of exercise, and that its water is always clean, fresh and cold to make it more appealing to drink, in order to prevent dehydration. In addition, brush your cat frequently to prevent hairballs, and have your kitty checked out by your vet if it seems to strain or is in pain while eliminating.

Urinary Tract Infection

Urinary Tract Infection is another common reason why cats do their business outside the box. Urinary Tract Infection, also known as UTI, is painful because it burns and stings when a cat urinates, and results in a cat only being able to produce a small amount of urination when it tries to go. Constipation can lead to a UTI because the pain of defecating can cause your feline to avoid the litter box and hold its pee which leads to infection.

UTI is more common in older cats, although any cat can get one, and is caused by a blocked urinary tract. Cats strain to go pee, leading owners to often mistake a UTI for constipation and miss what could be a serious medical emergency. If you notice that your cat is not producing much urine over several days, appears to be in pain when urinating, or is urinating outside the box, take it the vet right away and have it checked for a UTI.

The number one cause of Urinary Tract Infections is bacteria, although it can also be caused by fungus, parasites, viruses, urinary stones and even cancer. A bacterial UTI indicates that the cat's immune system is not functioning properly, allowing the bacteria to colonize and take hold in the form of an infection. A dirty litter box promotes bacteria and allows it to enter the cat's body through its urethra.

Your veterinarian will need to take a sample of your cat's urine in order to determine the cause of the UTI because this infection can also be indicative of an underlying health issue, such as diabetes, bladder stones or cancer. This is done by inserting a sterile syringe into your cat's bladder. If the UTI is caused by bacteria, your vet will prescribe antibiotics.

If your cat is prone to Urinary Tract Infections and you have ruled out any serious health issues, then you might want to consider only feeding it canned food since dehydration can lead to a UTI and there is 70 percent more moisture in wet food than dry. Also, make sure you always provide your cat with clean, fresh water every day – and keep the litter box clean!

Renal Failure

Peeing outside of the box could indicate that your cat is experiencing Renal Failure, also known as kidney failure. Other symptoms of possible Renal Failure include bacterial infections in the bladder and kidneys, weight loss, decreased appetite, vomiting, diarrhea, bloody or cloudy urine, mouth ulcers, bad breath, a brownish colored tongue, a dry coat, and constipation. When you combine these with your cat drinking more water than usual and urinating more than normal, than these are indications that your cat's kidneys are not working as well as they should be.

It is not unusual for a feline's kidneys to start failing as it ages. But if you suspect that your cat might have kidney problems, it is important to make an appointment with your vet. Kidney disease is treatable if caught early, but if it is left untreated, it can cause a host of health problems and become chronic, for which there is no cure.

There are two types of renal failure, both of which urinating outside the litter box could be a symptom of. *Acute Renal Failure* is not the result of age or of being born with faulty kidneys. Acute Renal Failure comes on quickly and is usually the result of ingesting something poisonous, trauma, rapid dehydration, kidney infection, kidney blockages, or heart failure with low blood pressure. If diagnosed early, Acute Renal Failure can be reversed.

Chronic Renal Failure, on the other hand, may be more difficult to treat. It is usually found in middle-aged or older cats and develops over months or years. Chronic Renal Failure, like acute kidney disease, can be the result of kidney infections and blockages that have worn down a cat's kidneys over time. Chronic Renal Failure can also be the result of poor dental health, cancer, hyperthyroidism, and high blood pressure.

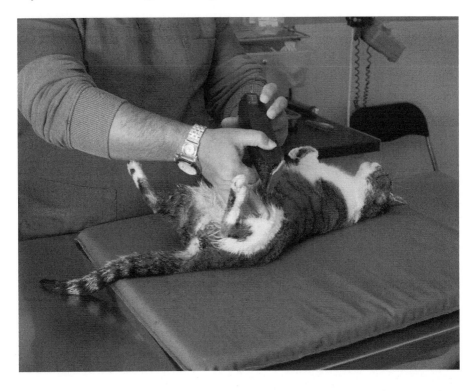

Treatments for Renal Failure can include surgery to remove any blockages, IV fluids, a special diet and medications. Your vet might advise you to feed your cat foods low in phosphorous and protein, but enriched with Vitamin D and omega 3 fatty acids. You will also need to provide your kitty with clean, fresh water, and schedule ongoing checkups with your vet to keep an eye on the disease. If Renal Failure is left untreated, it could prove fatal for your cat.

Cystitis

Cystitis, also known as Feline Lower Urinary Tract Disease (FLUTD), is an inflammation or infection of a cat's bladder, and can be acute, that is come on quickly, or it can be chronic, meaning long lasting. Cystitis can be caused by a bacterial infection or by urinary stones or crystals, and the pain accompanying it can lead many cats to stop using their litter boxes since they come to associate the pain with the box. In fact, Cystitis is the number one reason why cats stop using their litter boxes.

Cystitis affects more males than female cats, and diabetic cats are more prone to it since higher levels of glucose and protein in the urine encourage bacterial growth. Cystitis can also be caused by infrequent urination if your cat is avoiding its litter box for other reasons. Dehydration can also lead to Cystitis, and stress also plays a part in cats contracting the disease.

The symptoms of Cystitis often mimic Urinary Tract Infections, since it causes cats to strain during urination only to void minimal amounts of urine, or there is blood in your cat's urine, or excessive genital licking. Making frequent trips to the litter box or avoiding the litter box and urinating elsewhere, urine that has a strong odor, and crying when urinating are also common symptoms.

If your cat displays any of these signs, take it to your veterinarian right away. Failure to urinate can lead to death due to a bladder rupture or kidney failure! Your vet will check to see if your cat's bladder feels extended and may run some tests, such as a urinalysis, ultrasound, and bacteria culture. If your cat tests positive for Cystitis and it is the bacterial kind, then your vet will prescribe antibiotics. But if your cat has repeated cases of Cystitis, your vet might opt for surgery.

Once your cat has been treated, give it a diet mainly made up of canned food, since that contains moisture and dry food does not. Dry food often dehydrates cats and leads to conditions such as Cystitis. Also, avoid feeding your kitty fish flavored foods and make sure to always provide clear, fresh water to encourage your cat to drink more.

Urinary Tract Stones

Urinary Tract Stones is a condition that often leads to Cystitis mentioned above, which can cause a cat to urinate outside of the litter box. Urinary Tract Stones are also known as *uroliths*, and males are more susceptible to getting them than females, due to their longer urethra that can more easily get blocked. This makes urination very painful for a cat, who will often view the litter box as the source of its pain.

Uroliths can form in a cat's kidneys, but they usually form in the bladder. In addition to painful urination, uroliths can cause blood in the urine and cause your cat to attempt to urinate on a more frequent basis. Uroliths wind up blocking the urethra, making urination almost impossible. If your cat is having trouble urinating or seems in pain when voiding urine or you notice that there doesn't seem to be much urine in the litter box, or you suspect in any way that your cat has Urinary Tract Stones, take it to the veterinarian immediately. This is a medical emergency and could be a matter of life or death. Treatment will involve either dissolving the stones or surgery.

Declawing

There is another reason why declawing your cat is not a good idea, in addition to the fact that it is actually amputation of the first joint of a cat's toes on the front paws and removes a feline's ability to defend itself and to scratch an itch. Declawing can also lead to litter box elimination outside the box, a behavioral problem that sadly sees a lot of cats winding up at shelters.

When a cat is first declawed, the toe areas are very tender to the touch. Veterinarians usually instruct owners to use shredded newspaper instead of litter until the wounds heal. This causes confusion for many cats who do not like the change, and in rebellion, avoid the litter box.

In addition, cats who have been declawed often experience a life-long sensitivity in their feet, especially if a feline experiences lasting nerve damage after a declaw surgery. This can cause pain when a cat goes to cover up its waste, and often results in a cat either avoiding the litter box or never covering up its poop or pee.

Down in the Dumps

Depression is not just a human emotion. Cats and other animals can experience it too, but for them, depression can lower their immune system and lead to life threatening illnesses.

Why cats get depressed is as varied as why humans get the blues. Since felines hate change, a move to a new place, a new addition to the family, or a change in daily schedule are enough to make a cat depressed. Felines in animal shelters are often sad due to the confusion of being abandoned, not knowing why they are there, the inability to escape from the other cats in nearby cages, and the stress itself of living in a cage where its litter box is in close proximity to its food – something these fastidious animals simply cannot tolerate. It is not unusual for many cats in shelters to be so depressed that they get sick and die.

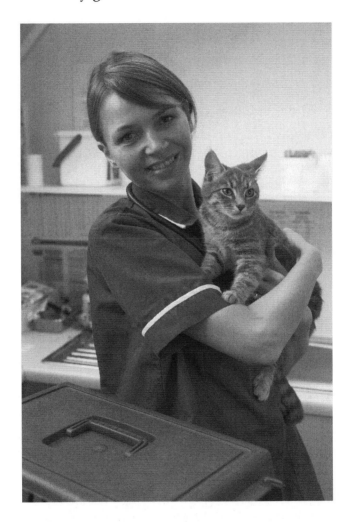

Cats are also highly sensitive to their owners' moods. If you are sad or stressed, your cat can pick up on this and take on your emotions, leading to depression.

It is not always easy to know that your cat is depressed if you are not paying attention. Loss of appetite is the most obvious sign, so if you find that your kitty is not eating, you might want to make an appointment with your veterinarian since undetected illnesses can also cause a cat to lose interesting in food.

If your cat is normally playful but is no longer interested, this could indicate depression. Or if you feline stops grooming or is grooming excessively, has a change in personality, or seems more aggressive than usual, these could be signs that your cat is depressed. And just like people, depressed cats sleep more than usual – not always easy to detect since cats sleep a good part of the day anyway. Hiding out of site for long periods of time can also warn of depression.

The best remedy for your cat's depression is to try to find the root of the problem. Have there been any changes to its world recently? Are you working longer hours at your job? Have you recently had someone new move in or had a baby or adopted a new pet? Have you recently lost another pet or a family member that your cat was fond of?

If you suspect that your cat is feeling down, try to spend more time with it – at least 30 minutes a day. Get some new cat toys that are mentally stimulating and make an effort to play with it every day. Remember to make time to groom and pet your cat, since touch can have healing effects. If you find that you are working more hours, leave a TV or radio on during the day. If your cat is an only cat, consider getting it a kitty friend.

Finally, take your cat to the vet for a complete checkup to make sure that the depression isn't masking a more serious illness. Cats who are depressed can become very sick, but illness can also cause depression. Your cat doesn't understand why it isn't feeling good and this can make it lethargic and sad. This is why it is important to make sure you consult with your vet so that your cat does not suffer.

Common Cat Diseases

Cats, like people, sometimes contract diseases that can be life threatening. Some of these diseases are similar to human illnesses of the same name, while others are unique to felines. Many of these diseases can mimic each other, which is why it is important to take your cat to your veterinarian if you notice that something is off with your cat's health or if your kitty develops unusual symptoms. Some diseases have no cures, but seek immediate veterinary help regardless. Being proactive with your feline's health could mean a matter of life or death, or may prevent unnecessary suffering.

Hyperthyroid disease

Hyperthyroidism is a common disease that attacks a cat's thyroid, causing an excessive concentration of the thyroidal hormone, thyroxine. Symptoms include dramatic weight loss, excessive thirst, increased urination, and an unquenchable appetite. Cats also become hyperactive, and may pant, suffer from diarrhea and vomiting, and shed more than normal amounts of fur.

Hyperthyroid disease can occur at any age, but most cats who suffer from Hyperthyroidism are between 12 and 13 years of age. Symptoms of Hyperthyroidism are similar to other diseases, such as Diabetes and kidney failure, and the disease is often fatal. While there are treatment options, all have their pros and cons and some can be expensive. These include administering an anti-thyroid medication, which is often effective but can have side effects; surgery to remove the thyroid gland, which is extremely expensive but effective, although there is always risks when surgery and anesthesia are involved; radioactive iodine therapy, which is probably the safest and most effective treatment, but is also expensive and involves boarding your cat for two to three weeks at your veterinarian's facility since your cat will be radio-active during this amount of time and that can be dangerous to you, your family, and other pets in your home.

Cancer

Cancer in cats can be hard to identify because felines often mask their illnesses. This often means that by the time cancer is detected, it may be at an advanced state, making it more difficult to treat and also more expensive.

While cats have a less chance of getting cancer than dogs, when they do get cancer, it is often a more aggressive form of the disease. Symptoms can include lumps, vomiting, diarrhea, skin conditions, bad breath, and difficulty breathing, or a cat might stop eating, have rapid, extreme weight loss, or appear lethargic. Since these symptoms can include other illnesses, it is always important to take your cat to the vet whenever something appears out of the ordinary.

Treatment for cancer often includes a biopsy, if possible, and then possibly surgery, followed by chemotherapy and/or radiation. But treating cancer in felines is also expensive, with a less than 50 percent survival rate. If an owner opts for no treatment, then pain relief and the eventual decision of euthanasia should be considered.

Preventing the disease is tricky, since cats are exposed to the same environmental hazards as humans are. However, spaying and neutering your cat, keeping it indoors, and certain vaccines can help to prevent many forms of feline cancer.

Diabetes

Diabetes in cats comes from consuming too many carbohydrates, which turn into sugar. If a cat's pancreas is unable to produce enough insulin to combat this sugar, it can lead to diabetes. Dry cat food, it should be noted, is often high in carbohydrates, and cats lack a liver enzyme needed to digest carbs. Wet cat food that specifies it is low in carbohydrates and is mainly made up of proteins, is the best option for cats.

Commercial foods, in fact, are one of the leading reasons why diabetes in cats is on the rise. Overfeeding our felines is another reason, especially if this overfeeding involves dry cat food. Symptoms of diabetes can mimic other feline illnesses, but include excessive thirst, increased urination, weight loss, loss of appetite or an insatiable appetite, vomiting, loss of motor functions, depression, coma and even death.

Diabetes can strike any cat, but being overweight increases the risks. Treatment involves daily insulin therapy, a low carbohydrate diet, and ongoing veterinary examinations and blood and urine tests. There is no cure for diabetes, but it can be controlled. While some cats go into remission, it is a chronic disease that must be monitored for the lifetime of the cat.

Feline Leukemia

Feline Leukemia, also known as FeLV, is a virus that is shed in saliva and nasal secretions, but can also be passed via the urine, feces and milk of infected felines. Transfer of the virus can be spread from an infected cat to an uninfected one through bites, mutual grooming, and dishes, and is prevalent in animal shelters and among cats that are allowed to roam.

FeLV is, in fact, a leading cause of cancer among felines. It can also cause blood disorders and lower a cat's immune system, making it susceptible to other diseases and illnesses. Cats may not show any symptoms during the early stages of the virus, but over time FeLV will deteriorate a cat's health. Eventually, a cat may exhibit a loss of appetite, weight loss, a dull or matty coat, enlarged lymph nodes, fever, pale gums or inflammation of the gums, skin infections, bladder or upper respiratory infections, persistent diarrhea, and seizures.

FeLV is diagnosed through blood tests, which can sometimes produce a false positive and why it is important to get a second blood test if your cat tests positive. Prevention includes keeping your cat indoors, having a cat tested for the virus before adopting it, and making sure your cat receives a FeLV vaccine – although the vaccine is not fool proof, which is why it is important for many reasons to make your cat an indoor cat. Unfortunately, 85 percent of cats who are infected with the Feline Leukemia virus die within three years of contracting the disease. On the other hand, 70 percent of healthy cats are able to ward of contracting the virus.

Heart disease

Cardiomyopathy is the most common heart condition found in cats. The word literally means, "disease of the heart muscle," and accounts for two thirds of the heart diseases found in felines. It usually affects a cat's left heart ventricle and rarely affects the right, in which the heart chamber becomes thickened, scarred or dilated.

If left untreated, Cardiomyopathy can lead to progressive heart failure, fluid in and around the lungs, and respiratory distress. It also can cause paralysis causing blood clots that can lodge in arteries, particularly arteries in the rear legs, resulting in sudden death.

Often, Cardiomyopathy is genetic, but it can result from other diseases such as hyperthyroidism. Symptoms include difficulty with breathing or walking. If your cat exhibits either of these, it is imperative that you take it to your vet right away. Your veterinarian will first rule out hyperthyroid disease, hypertension, anemia, or high blood pressure. Usually, treating these conditions will take care of the heart disease as well. If these are ruled out, your vet will do a chest scan. If it is determined that your cat has Cardiomyopathy or another heart condition, your vet will prescribe medicine, although this does not necessarily prevent blood clots. Heart disease is a chronic disease that can sometimes be controlled with medicine, but eventually a cat will succumb to the condition.

Parasites

Most cats will experience a parasite or two at some point in their lives. Some parasites are merely irritating, while others can be life threatening. But all parasites have the ability to carry disease and transmit those from cat to humans or other pets.

Some parasites, like *Cheyletiella* mites, fleas and ear mites, are more nuisance than dangerous. Cheyletiella mites live on a cat's skin, causing an itchy rash and skin irritations. Fleas also irritate cats and can be difficult to eradicate. Fleas can jump from cats to humans to other pets in the home, causing a miserable cycle of itchy and painful irritation. Ear mites live in a cat's ear canal, causing severe irritation and itchiness inside the ears.

Other parasites use cats and other pets in order to complete their life cycles from egg to larvae to adult and as a place to lay their eggs. *Cuterebra* parasites are one such opportunistic organism that completes its life cycle under a cat's skin, often undetected. While Cuterebra parasites are not life threatening, they can cause secondary illnesses.

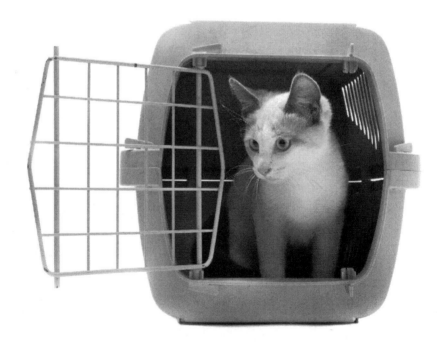

Giardia is a one-celled parasite that lives in a cat's intestinal tract and can cause diarrhea. Heartworms are transmitted to cats via mosquitoes and live mainly in the lungs and heart. Heartworm disease is difficult to treat and can be fatal, but heartworm medicine can prevent this parasite from taking hold.

Hookworms are one of the most common parasites found in cats, and hook themselves onto a cat's intestinal tract where they feed off blood and tissue, often moving around the intestines. Hookworms can be passed to humans. They are not life threatening, but can cause ulcers and diarrhea. Whipworms are also intestinal parasites found mainly in dogs, but can affect cats. They also feed on blood. Ringworms, on the other hand, are not a worm but a fungus that forms under a cat's skin, causing a lesion that can be passed to humans.

Ticks are perhaps the most dangerous of parasites, affecting cats, dogs and humans. Ticks cause Lyme disease which can be fatal or cause life time health issues.

If your cat is allowed to go outside, it is more susceptible to contracting a parasite. Check your feline daily for ticks, and have it tested for all parasites annually by your veterinarian.

Upper respiratory infection

Upper Respiratory Infection (URI) is actually a variety of infections derived from viruses or bacteria that can affect a cat's nose, throat and sinus area. URIs is passed from cat to cat, making outdoor felines and cats at shelters or pet stores especially susceptible. Once a cat gets a URI, it becomes a carrier for life and can transmit the infection through sneezing, coughing, grooming other cats, and shared food and water bowls.

Common symptoms of URIs include sneezing, nasal congestion, nasal discharges, gagging, drooling, fever, loss of appetite, nasal and mouth ulcers, squinting, rubbing eyes, and depression. Stress can make cats more susceptible to picking up URIs, such as the stress many cats feel in shelters, and once a cat has acquired a URI, it is more likely to come down with it again when under stress.

If you suspect that your cat might have an Upper Respiratory Infection, take it to your vet right away to prevent your cat from spreading the infection. Treatments can antibiotics, intravenous fluids, antiviral medications, eye ointment, and specific nutritional plans. Left untreated, URI can lead to pneumonia, chronic breathing difficulties, and even blindness.

You can prevent your cat from acquiring this infection by keeping it indoors, and by vaccinating it against Upper Respiratory Infection. The URI vaccine may not entirely prevent your cat from catching this disease, but it can lessen the severity should your cat acquire a URI. Also, feed your cat a healthy diet and schedule yearly visits to the vet. A healthy immune system is a cat's best defense against a URI.

Feline Aids

Feline Aids, also known as Feline Immunodeficiency Virus Infection or FIV, is a retrovirus that suppresses a cat's immune system. It can be prevented by making sure your cat receives an FIV vaccine.

FIV can lay dormant in your cat for years with no health problems. Once your cat's immune system is compromised, however, it may display symptoms such as a recurrence of minor illnesses such as upper respiratory infections, enlarged lymph nodes, inflamed gums, eye diseases, persistent diarrhea, chronic kidney problems, recurrent ear and skin infections, poor coat condition, fever, wasting away of body fat, vision and hearing problems, and nerve disorders in the legs and paws.

FIV is transmitted through bite wounds and scratches, and can be detected through blood tests and urinalysis. Your veterinarian will first try to control secondary infections because your cat's suppressed immune system can make it easy for other infections and diseases to wreck havoc on your cat's health. Your kitty may need surgery if its gums are infected or tumors are detected, and your vet may put your cat on a special diet to boost its immune system.

You will need to continue to monitor your cat's health once it is home. You may also need to quarantine your cat if you have other cats and make sure they receive the FIV vaccine. By staying on top of the disease, you cat can live a long a healthy life.

Feline infectious peritonitis

Feline Infectious Peritonitis or FIP is a viral infection that is usually fought off by a feline's immune systems. But sometimes it develops into Feline Infectious Peritonitis Virus or *clinical* FIP, affecting a cat's white blood cells which then transport the virus to other parts of its body. This results in an intense inflammatory reaction around vessels located in the abdomen, kidneys or brain. Once a cat develops clinical FIP, the disease is progressive and almost always fatal.

Luckily, FIP is not highly contagious. However, it is passed cat-to-cat, through an infected cat's feces and saliva, so any cat exposed to it can pick up the disease. The virus can also exist in the environment for several weeks, so cats who are allowed to roam can cross paths with this infection. FIP is also passed from infected mother cats to their kittens, whose under developed immune systems make them susceptible to contagion.

Initially, cats that contract clinical FIP show no symptoms, although some might exhibit sneezing, watery eyes, nasal discharge or diarrhea. But once the FIP virus kicks in, it may appear that a cat suddenly comes down with FIP, when in reality it probably was masking the symptoms for some time or had no symptoms. When FIP reaches this crisis state, a cat may have no appetite, experience dramatic weight loss, poor coat condition, depression and fever, eventually ending in death. FIP can be difficult to diagnose since these symptoms are similar to those displayed with other feline diseases.

Unfortunately, there is no diagnostic test for FIP, nor has there been much success the development of a preventative vaccine. Tests that exist only indicate that a cat has been exposed to the virus, not that it has the disease. However, should your cat exhibit any of the above mentioned symptoms, take it to your vet right away since these could indicate any number of feline illnesses or diseases.

Feline distemper

Feline Panleukopenia, more commonly known as Feline Distemper or FPV, is a highly contagious, life threatening disease that affects rapidly dividing bloods cells, particularly in the intestinal tract and bone marrow and in the stem cells of kitten fetuses. This can lead to anemia and susceptibility to contract other diseases.

The best way to prevent FPV is through vaccination since the disease can survive in the environment for years. If a cat manages to survive FPV, it will be immune from contracting it again. Symptoms include vomiting, bloody diarrhea, dehydration, weight loss, fever, anemia, poor hair coat, depression, lack of appetite, hanging head over water or food dish but not drinking or eating, feet tucked under the body for long periods of time, chin resting on floor for long periods of time, and lack of coordination or clumsiness.

Cats can contract FPV through infected feces, blood, urine or fleas, and from people who have not washed their hands after handling infected cats. It can also remain on surfaces where infected cats have been. This is why it is important to keep your cat indoors, and to be careful where you board your cat when you are out of town.

FPV can mimic other diseases, so it is important to take your cat to your vet immediately should you suspect it is ill. Your vet will run blood tests and urinalysis, as well as a biochemistry file. If your vet determines your cat has FPV, it will be given fluids, since dehydration can be life threatening, as well as antibiotics in order to prevent other opportunistic diseases from attacking your cat. You will also need to isolate your cat from other pets in your home until it is well again. The best prevention for FPV in the first place is a distemper or FPV vaccine.

Typical Warning Signs of Sickness

Cats are pros at hiding illnesses, a habit that probably dates back to their wild ancestors when illness could make them vulnerable to predators. By the time you notice that your cat doesn't seem itself, it has probably been sick for a while.

Kitty cannot tell you that it isn't feeling well, but it does communicate illness in other ways. As mentioned earlier in the chapter, many feline diseases and illnesses mimic each other, so prompt veterinary care is essential. Here are some warning signs you should be aware of, some of which may be red flags while others that should be taken in conjunction with other symptoms.

Lethargy

When cats seem lethargic, there is a pretty good chance it is not well. Lethargy can include drowsiness, no energy, slow to react, or sleeping more than usual. If your cats show these signs for more than a day or two, make an appointment with your vet. Anemia, system disorders, injury or cancer are some of the illnesses that can make your cat lethargic.

Repetitive vomiting or gagging

Most cats wind up vomiting from time to time to throw up hairballs when they have ingested too much fur. But some cats eat foreign objects, such as string, thread or other items they find irresistible for some reason, and repetitive vomiting or gagging could indicate an obstruction in their esophagus, stomach or intestines that could be life threatening. Recurring vomiting or gagging can also indicate a serious illness, such as kidney disease. Make an appointment with your veterinarian immediately, especially if your cat is not eating, drinking or going to the bathroom.

Stops eating

If your cat's eating habits change drastically, this should be a cause of concern. It could be a sign of a serious disease or a reaction to a recent vaccine. It might also indicate a urinary tract infection or renal failure. If your cat has lost its appetite and it does not resume after a day or two, make a vet appointment right away.

Diarrhea

Cats have occasional diarrhea, especially if they have eaten people food or have consumed milk or other dairy products. But diarrhea can also indicate disease, allergies, worms, or an allergic reaction. Limit your cat's food intake, but if the diarrhea doesn't clear up or appears black or bloody, you will want to pay a visit to the vet.

Blood in the urine

If you notice blood in your cat's litter box after it has urinated, this could indicate cancer or blood clots. It also might mean kidney failure or urinary tract infection, so get it checked out by your vet for peace of mind.

Sudden weight loss or weight gain

It is one thing to overfeed your feline and have it get chubby, or put your overweight cat on a diet and witness it losing weight over time. But if the weight gain or loss is sudden, this could indicate cancer, hyperthyroid disease, diabetes, gastrointestinal problems, parasites, viruses, or any number of other health problems. Make a veterinary appointment immediately.

Drinking more water and urinating more frequently

If you find that you are filling up your cat's water bowl more often or scooping more urine out of the litter box, keep a close eye on the situation. Diabetes, kidney problems and hyperthyroid disease increase a cat's thirst and the need to urinate more often. Make an appointment with your vet in order to test for these and other deadly diseases.

Gum changes

Red or swollen gums can lead to gum disease, which over time can be fatal for a cat. Gum problems can also cause a cat to lose its teeth, making it impossible to eat. Have your cat's teeth and gums checked annually by your vet who might recommend teeth cleaning or a cat toothpaste that can keep your cat's teeth clean and prevent gum disease.

Runny eyes or nose

If your cat has discharges from its eyes or nose, take it to the vet right away. This could be an indicator of allergies, a respiratory infection or serious illness, especially if accompanied by wheezing, sneezing and shortness of breath.

Shortness of breath, panting or coughing

If it appears that your cat is having a difficult time breathing or it has a persistent cough, make a vet appointment immediately. Cats cannot sweat to cool themselves, so panting is a sign that your cat is in respiratory distress. Shortness of breath or coughing could be an indicator of dehydration, toxicity, asthma, respiratory disease, cancer or other serious health issues.

Stiffness when moving

Cats, like people, stiffen up from arthritis as they age. But stiffness or difficulty in walking and moving can also indicate muscle atrophy and neurological problems. Have your cat checked by your vet just to play it safe.

Ear itching

If you notice that your cat is constantly scratching its ears, shaking its head, has a brown excretion coming from and around the ears, and the ears are in a steady position of "airplane ears," that is down and flat, this could indicate ear mites. Ear mites and the constant scratching that pursues can be painful for your cat, plus if left untreated, can cause ear vessels to rupture and lead to hearing loss. In addition, ear mites are highly contagious, so if you have more than one cat, they can be passed from kitty to kitty. While there are ear mite products, have your veterinarian check your cat's ears just to play it safe. Persistent ear scratching could also indicate illness, plus some ear mite products can burn your cat's ears if too much is put in the ears.

Fever

A cat's normal body temperature is around 101 degrees. Anything over 102.5 should be a cause for concern, especially if your cat's nose is warm to the touch. Take your cat in to your vet immediately, since temperatures over 106 degrees can cause organ damage. Fevers can be caused by infections, tumors, recent trauma, a reaction from medicine, or serious diseases.

Lumps or abnormal growths

If you notice a lump or growth on your cat, have it checked by your veterinarian. This could be an indicator of cancer, an infected cat bite, hernia, cysts or tumors. In fact, always have any changes to your cat's body checked out.

Disorientation

Like people, a cat's cognitive ability diminishes slightly with age. But if your cat seems to be confused by routine tasks, doesn't recognize you or people its familiar with, appears to be walking around in a daze, stops using its litter box or uses odd places to eliminate, has trouble with obstacles in its way, or starts making unfamiliar sounds, have it checked by your vet immediately. Cats can become disorientated when they have had a stroke or brain tumor, or have a neurological disorder or cognitive dysfunction syndrome.

Back leg dragging or paralysis

If you notice that your cat's rear legs seem paralyzed or that your cat is dragging its back legs, get it to the vet immediately. This could be a sign of a blood clot being passed from its heart to lungs or a sign of kidney failure.

Matty coat or skin changes

When a cat stops grooming or you notice coat or skin changes, this could be a cause for concern. Cats often stop grooming when they have an illness such as hyperthyroidism, are feeling under the weather, have neurological problems, or some other serious ailment. They also excessively lick their hair off and bite their skin when they have had an allergic reaction or are being tormented by fleas or mites. Make a vet appointment right away.

Play it safe

It should be noted that whenever you see a change in your cat's condition or behavior that seems out of the ordinary, it is always a good idea to make a vet appointment. It may be something minor, such as stress from a change in your household, or it could indicate a serious or life threatening illness. When it comes to your cat's wellbeing, it is always best to play it safe and seek medical attention.

Teaching Your Cat
the Rules of the House

C ats are like children – if you don't teach them
the rules of your home, they will decide on
the rules themselves. Training your cat to
understand what is and is not acceptable ensures a home life
that is free of chaos and provides a peaceful coexistence with
your feline.

Cats are all about tranquility since stress can lead to bad behavior, such as a litter box problems, and even illness. Nothing promotes a happy home life for your cat than order, boundaries and
rules. Even if your cat appears to want to run the show, this can
only lead to destructive habits. But in order to communicate the
rules of your home effectively, you must first understand how a
cat learns.

Learning to Learn

Cats are not obedient creatures by nature. They do not have a pack mentality, as dogs do, so there is no need for a cat to be submissive to another cat or human who is higher in the hierarchy or pecking order. Cats, in fact, have to be taught how to learn in order to understand what the rules of your home are. They do not learn in order to please, but rather, they learn to improve their lives.

Cats are self-motivated learners who master rules when it is in their best self interests. In other words, if you want to teach your cat to behave, you have to prove to it that the rules are beneficial. You do this by showing a cat that a cause has an effect, that is, if they behave in the way you want it to, the reward is a treat or praise. For cats, there has to be a predictable outcome. When owners unknowingly reward their cats for acting out, such as feeding it on demand, then their cats learn to be insistent about being fed, since they know that their owners will relent.

Make the lesson fun

If you want your cat to learn the rules of your home, you have to make your training fun and not a lesson in discipline. Cats learn by experience, so be prepared to be repetitious – and patient. If the experience is a good one, such as ending in a reward such as a treat or praise, then cats are more likely to repeat it. If you want to break a bad habit, on the other hand, then you want the experience to be unpleasant. Cats very rarely try anything twice if the first time is a negative one.

This means that you do not want to reward your cat for behavior you find irritating or obnoxious. For example, a common complaint among many cat owners is that their cats wake them up early in the morning, demanding to be fed. Many people will then get up and feed their cats just to get their felines to leave them alone. This, however, rewards their cats and teaches them to repeat this action.

Treats are a great way to train your cat and break bad habits because your cat learns in no time that by behaving a certain way will mean a tasty reward. For example, say you have purchased a scratching post, but your cat prefers clawing your furniture. Whenever you see your cat scratching the couch or furniture, say "no!" in a loud, firm voice and then pick up your cat and bring it over to the scratching post. Next, take your cat's front paws, scratch them on the post, praise your kitty, and then give it a treat. Repeat this every time you see your cat scratching a piece of furniture to reinforce using the post. Soon, your cat will associate the furniture with the loud "no," and the post with praise and a treat.

Also, every time you see your feline scratching the post *on its own* without any prompts from you, praise it and reward it with a treat. Once again, your cat will link the scratching post with something good to eat. It should be noted that until your cat changes its behavior about scratching the furniture, keep the room that the furniture is in off limits by closing the door. Clawed up fabric and scratched up furniture tempt cats to further scratch them, so do not encourage this behavior by allowing your cat access to it. After a while, your cat will trade the furniture for the scratching post in order to receive praise or treats.

You will also need to make access to a scratching post easy for your cat by placing several scratching posts in different rooms throughout your home. Often, owners make the mistake of only owning one post and then when their cat claws up the furniture, they throw up their hands and claim that their kitty won't use a post. Think about it from a cat's perspective: if your cat is in one room and feels the urge to scratch, it isn't going to say to itself, "Hey, I think I'll go into the next room and use the scratching post that is in there." Instead, it will use whatever is readily available, such as the nearby furniture or drapes.

If you want your cat to stop jumping up on the kitchen counter, bathroom vanity, table or even your bed, and you can see that it is ready to make the leap, say "no!" in a loud, firm voice and then give your cat a treat when it complies. If your cat is already on the counter, do not reward it with a treat after it has jumped down. That will reinforce the idea that if it jumps on the counter, it will be rewarded with a treat.

If your cat has been avoiding the litter box, first make sure it isn't a health issue. If it isn't, then find out why your placement of the litter box is causing your cat stress. Cats always have a reason for eliminating outside the box – they don't do it just to be bad

– and this is their way to communicate it. Try moving the box to another location and see if that breaks the habit. Praise your cat and reward it with a treat whenever you see it going in the box. Also, give your cat time each day for your undivided attention and to play with it. Cats who feel neglected often protest by not using their boxes.

If you do not want your cat to access a certain room, be consistent with this rule. Don't let your cat in the room some times, and other times refuse them entry. Cats tend to want what they cannot have, and this will only encourage the desire to somehow get in that room. Cats have been known to tear up carpet or even scratch up a door in an attempt to get into a room they have gone in before and now are being told they can't. Either your cat is allowed in a room or it isn't, so make sure everyone in your family is on board. When your cat asks to enter the room, tell it, "no!" and then give it a treat.

On the other hand, if you are trying to clean your home or are trying to concentrate on a project, for example, and your cat is pestering you, do not reward your kitty by stopping and petting it. Give a firm, "no," and gently push it away. Also, don't pet your cat if it is doing something you do not want it to do. By stopping what you are doing or petting your cat when it is behaving badly only reinforces the behavior.

Make sure your home environment is one where your cat is not being rewarded for misbehaving. Reward and praise the good behavior, which will make the negative behavior less appealing. Be consistent with your commands so that you can set your cat up to succeed. Have well defined boundaries regarding where your cat can and cannot go, and what it is allowed and not allowed to do. In addition, make sure you correct your cat's bad behavior within the first few seconds it occurs. If you wait until later, your cat will not be able to make the connection between the cause and effect and you won't get the results you want.

If you know your cat is behaving badly but you never seem to be around to catch it in the act, you can set up deterrents. For example, if you see evidence that your cat jumps on the kitchen counter, but you never actually see it do it, use double stick tape and leave it on the counter. It is harmless, but your cat won't appreciate having to get it unstuck from its fur. More than likely, your cat will avoid the kitchen counter after that since cats will avoid unpleasant experiences.

Never, ever yell at or punish your cat. This will only teach your cat to run away and could result in it acting out in negative ways. It can also create stress, which is the leading cause of problem behavior in cats, and can compromise their immune systems, which in turn can lead to illness. It will also destroy your cat's trust in you. Remember, there are no bad cats, only owners who badly train them.

Feeding on Your Time – Not Your Cat's

Cats prefer consistency in their lives. Variations upset and stress them. But they also are motivated by food, so be sure you are the one – and not your cat – who controls the feeding times. Free-feeding your cat can also lead to weight gain, which can result in disease. Keep a set schedule of when your cat gets fed, and then make sure you stick to it.

Cats are great at pestering their owners until their owners finally give in. They are also good at begging for more food, even when they are no longer hungry. Instead of folding under the pressure of the persistent meow, distract your cat with other activities.

Not only will you be training your cat about eating times, but you will be benefiting its health.

One great way to do this is to get a feeder toy, such as a ball with a single hole where you place treats or a small amount of dry food. This allows you to put a small amount of food inside the toy and then the cat has to work at getting it out. When your cat bats the ball around, the treats drop out, which not only can satisfy your cat's desire to eat, but also appeal to its natural hunt and catch nature.

Try very hard to stick to a schedule about your cat's feeding times. Even if your cat is bugging you to feed it, consistency means stability to your cat. If your cat wakes you up in the morning, do not get up to feed it unless this is its normal time to eat. By giving in and getting up, you are reinforcing this behavior. If your cat pesters you to feed it every time you walk into the kitchen, chase it out or get what you need and leave, but do not give in to its demands. If you work a crazy schedule, then consider getting an automatic feeder that distributes a set amount of food over a period of time.

Of course, it is impossible for cats to understand when time changes during daylight savings time or when it reverts back to normal time in the fall, and this throws their whole schedule off. During the times of year when the clocks move forward or back, gradually ease your cat into its new schedule. Do this by feeding your cat a little bit later each day during the fall when your cat is used to eating according to the daylight savings time schedule and now must wait an hour later so that its body and inner clock adjust to the new time.

Also, do not allow your cat to be a picky eater. While it is true that, like people, cats have individual tastes, the truth is that cats do not mind eating the same food they like day after day after day. Unlike people, they do not need variety. Choose a well balanced diet of high quality food, and then stick to that brand and flavor. Switching up the brands not only confuses your cat, it can lead to finicky eating habits. The only reason you should ever change your cat's food is if you discover something unhealthy or bad about the food you were feeding it or if your cat develops a health problem that requires it to be on a special diet prescribed by your veterinarian.

If your cat is calling the shots about its food, do the 20 minute plan. Give your cat 20 minutes to eat its food, but if it turns up its nose and doesn't eat after this time frame, remove the food until your cat's next eating time. If your cat acts hungry before then, give it the same food. Do not switch it out for something else – doing so will only reinforce its picky behavior.

It can be difficult to resist the insistent meows of a hungry cat who demands to be fed before feeding time. As hard as it can be, ignore its persistence or you will set yourself and your cat up for a free-for-all eating pattern. If you give in, your cat will know that this tactic will work whenever it wants to be fed.

Also, make sure to coordinate your cat's eating times at the same time as yours, if possible. Otherwise, you could wind up with a cat who wants to join you for dinner, and who will pester you and your family during your mealtimes. Make sure you give your cat its food a few minutes before you sit down for yours. This way, your kitty won't be distracted by your meal because it will be focused on eating its own food.

In addition, make sure you do not feed your cat human table scraps. This not only sets up your cat to be a beggar, it can upset its nutritional balance. Feeding your cat human food can also lead to obesity, contribute to your cat's finicky eating habits, and even cause health problems since human food is often too rich and spicy for cats.

Finally, if you find that feeding your cat twice a day doesn't seem to satisfy it, try feeding it several smaller meals, as long as you do this at set times. Also, make sure to measure the amount out so that your cat doesn't gain weight.

Don't Discipline – Discourage

Disciplining a cat when it acts out or misbehaves is just as counterproductive as rewarding a cat for bad behavior. This might seem to run in opposition with the fact that a cat will not repeat an unpleasant experience, but when it comes to a cat acting out in a negative way, the punishment, if you will, not only must fit the crime – it must be administered the second the crime is committed. Otherwise, the only results you will achieve are confusing your cat and having your cat think you cannot be trusted.

Breaking a cat's bad habit can be difficult because it is nearly impossible to catch a cat in the act. It is futile to discipline your cat once the deed is done because your kitty will not make the connection between your displeasure and the evidence left behind of its misdeed. For example, say your cat has peed on the carpet. Grabbing your cat and showing it the wet spot putting its nose in it, then dragging your cat over to the litter box and then digging its paws into the litter, will not make your cat realize that it should have urinated in the box and not on the carpet. All you will succeed at doing is training your cat to avoid you when you go to grab it and teaching it that the litter box is an unpleasant experience. Besides, cats act out for a reason – in this case, a cat will only eliminate outside the litter box because something is wrong, such as it has a urinary tract infection or the box needs to be clean. A cat will *not* go to the bathroom outside of the box just to spite you!

Even when you catch your cat in the act of doing something wrong, reprimanding or yelling at it will not achieve the results you are hoping for. Your cat is misbehaving because it either is trying to tell you something is wrong or it is seeking your attention. Disciplining your cat just teaches your cat to mistrust you or reinforces the bad behavior because it gives your cat the attention it wants.

So how do you discourage your cat from misbehaving? First, give your cat more attention, take time to play with it, and make your relationship a fun and loving one. Next, set up your cat to succeed by rewarding your cat when it is behaving or has mastered the behaviors you want it to learn. Cats learn by treats or praise, and your cat will connect good behavior with pleasure.

Also, make it easy for your cat to follow the rules. Make sure you place a scratching post in each room so that your cat can choose that instead of your furniture or drapes. If you have more than one story in your home or more than one cat, provide a litter box on each floor or for each cat. Keep the litter box clean and change it often. Keep doors closed to rooms you do not want your cat in and make sure that all family members do the same. The bottom line is, be consistent. Your cat won't know what the rules are if you enforce them some of the time and not at other times.

Make sure to never, ever yell at your cat, and never, ever hit it. Felines are very sensitive and if you hurt your cat's feelings or lose your temper or physically discipline it, your cat won't understand why and therefore it won't trust you. Saying a command in a firm but level tone is not the same thing as yelling. Use your high voice when you want to express affection or instigate play or when you call your cat's name. Use a lower but calm tone to let your cat know when you are displeased about its behavior.

Also, step back and try to figure out if there is a reason why your cat is misbehaving. If its routine has changed, your cat might be upset and this is the only way it can communicate its feelings. Perhaps your cat is lonely if it is your only cat and is left alone all day. Consider getting it another cat friend so that it has company while you are gone. Also, take a look around your home and view it from your cat's perspective. If the litter box is difficult to get to, or its food is in a heavy traffic area, your cat might act out in order to get your attention to the problem.

Finally, remember that your cat's behavior is really a reflection of you. Your cat will follow your lead, but it has to know what you expect. It also needs your time and attention – by keeping its litter box and food area clean, by knowing you will spend time playing with it, and by taking time to pet and groom it. If you cat's behavior isn't up to your standards, chances are your own behavior or unrealistic expectations are the reasons why.

Drawing the Line Between Play and Aggression

Cats are independent animals, but that doesn't mean they don't want and need interaction. Play is not simply a mindless activity. It stimulates your cat on so many levels. Playtime plays into your feline's inherited need to hunt and catch prey. It also is mentally and physically stimulating, and it creates a bond between you and your kitty, and your cat and other felines in your home.

This is why it is so important to take the time to play with your cat at least one or two times each day. Your cat needs and loves interacting with you, and when you ignore this, your cat will be unhappy and even depressed. This can lead to acting out in your cat's attempts to catch your attention. Negative attention to your cat is better than no attention at all.

Aggressive behavior is one that you want to discourage in your cat, but you need to be able to tell the difference between when your cat is acting aggressively and when it is merely playing. If your cat silently "attacks" your legs as you walk by but doesn't break your skin, that's play. Grabbing your leg while sinking its front claws into your skin and using its back feet and claws to scratch up your skin causing you to bleed is an act of aggression and should not be tolerated. Often this form of aggression includes your cat hissing or growling and may even include your cat biting you or another pet. If your cat acts this way, clap your hands and say, "no," but then figure out why your cat is upset. It may have to do with recent changes in your household, such as a new pet or baby, or a change in your cat's routine. If the issue involves the recent introduction of a new cat or other pet, keep the two separate until your cat gets used to the new addition, but also be sure to spend extra time with your cat.

It may be difficult not to get angry with your cat when it has painfully wounded you or acts in an aggressive manner. But it is important to figure out what brought about your kitty's aggression, so that you can resolve the issue. If you haven't been spending time with your cat or if you haven't taken the proper and patient steps needed in introducing a new addition to your family, this is your feline's way of letting you know it is upset and you need to be the one to fix the problem.

This is especially important if your cat's behavior is not its normal way of acting. In addition to a new pet or new person in the home, a recent change of residence or a change in your cat's environment, or not enough time spent together, your cat could be upset by loud noises in your neighborhood or a recent loud storm, an encounter with another aggressive cat or dog if your cat is allowed outdoors, or houseguests who are upsetting your cat's normal routine.

In any case, if your cat's play seems a little too aggressive, or if it is acting out in an aggressive way, try to remedy the situation by distracting it through games that involve hunting and catching prey, such as having your cat chase you as you run with a string, allowing it to catch it once in a while, or tossing a small ball or mouse at your cat so that it can bat it around, or perhaps the most favorite cat game of all – having it chase the red laser dot. Also, make sure that you do not encourage aggressive play by swatting at your cat or using your hands and feet as toys. If you do that, then your cat will respond by swatting or biting back. In addition, pay attention to your cat's signals that it has had enough of your game or petting. Failure to recognize the cues, which can include your cat hissing or turning its back or meowing loudly, could result in it telling you to stop in the only way it knows how – with a bite or scratch.

A bored cat is an unhappy cat

Boredom is one of the leading causes of bad behavior in cats, and the fault lies with the owners. Cats are highly intelligent creatures, which means they need to be mentally stimulated and physically challenged. When that doesn't happen, a cat will find a way to amuse itself, even if the stimulation comes in the form of destructive behavior.

In fact, most behavioral problems are either the result of a litter box that is not clean or is in a highly trafficked area where the cat has little privacy, or because a cat is bored and unhappy and this is its way of communicating those feelings to you. This can also be a health issue, since a cat that is happy and mentally and physically stimulated will also be healthier. It doesn't take much to make a difference in your cat's life. Cats have short attention spans, so ten or 15 minutes of fun games like chasing a string on the end of a wand or a red dot from a laser toy or batting around a ball or mouse you have tossed your cat's way a few times a day is really all it will take to make your cat a happy, well adjusted kitty. Best of all, by playing with your cat, you will deepen the bond between you, which will be enriching for both your cat and you.

When you are at work or not around, create an environment that also keeps your cat from getting bored. Consider getting another cat companion so that your cat has someone to hang out with. Play soft music on the radio or turn the TV on at a low volume to keep your cat from getting lonely. Buy a cat perch and place it near a window so that your feline can watch birds and other outdoor creatures from the safety of your home. Place some of your cat's favorite toys around but be sure to rotate them since cats are easily bored.

Keep in mind that when you create this stimulating environment for your cat, it is no replacement for your company and for playing with your cat. Felines are social creatures and they are happiest when interacting with their people. The time you invest in playing, interacting and spending quality time with your cat will pay off in good behavior, trust and a loving relationship between you two.

Funny Antics – Why Cats Can Be Amusing, Hilarious, Endearing ... and Infuriating!

ats make excellent companions. And there is no doubt that they enjoy being our pets. But every cat owner will tell you that their cat has some funny, engaging and even a little odd behaviors that go beyond explanation. Perhaps that is why we find them so enjoyable – we never know what to expect from our cats. From sleeping in odd places, to choosing strange items as toys, to waking us up on cue, to being able to open doors, and more, cats keep us entertained and amused.

Sleep Gymnastics

There are cats that sleep with their owners every night. Perhaps your cat is your faithful sleep companion. But most cats like to switch things up, and no one is quite sure why. You might find your cat sleeping in all the usual places, but every once in a while come across it taking a nap in the oddest of locales. It is also not unusual to not be able to find your cat at bedtime, only to have it saunter out in the morning with no clue of where it spent the night.

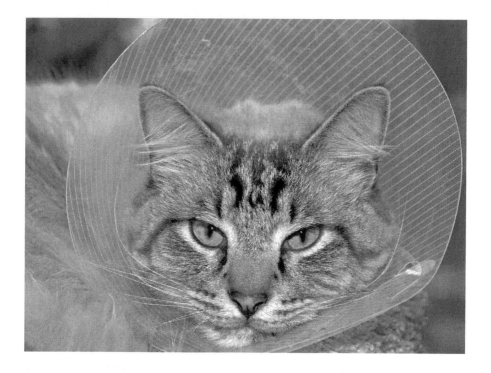

Cats, in fact, can sleep anywhere. They are experts when it comes to taking naps. Often, they will seek out a sunny window or a cushiony couch or chair or the comfort of a bed. Sometimes they do not mind sleeping out in the open, without a care of who is walking and talking around it. Other times, they prefer privacy, and will seek out an area out of the way. Cats have been known to sleep on dining room chairs, only to be discovered when someone pulls one out to sit. Sometimes a feline might desire the enclosed, safe feeling of a box or basket or some other small space. This is why it is very important to keep doors closed on washers and dryers and lids fastened on any item that might endanger a napping cat should someone not know it is sleeping there.

Cats also sleep in weird positions. Sometimes it is the usual cat pose where it is curled up with its tail wrapped around it, or it may prefer lying sprawled out on its side. But sometimes your cat may fall asleep in a position that defies comfort, such as lying on its back with its four feet in the air. While each cat has its own preferred sleeping position – and many have more than one – there are some common sleep poses that many cats find comfy.

Blocking out the world

You have probably seen your cat sleeping with one paw over its face, hiding its eyes. This is your cat's way of saying it does not want to be petted or bothered in any way while it is trying to catch some Zs. Your cat might also do this if a nearby light or the sun is too bright and it doesn't want to make an effort to find a darker place to sleep. Or maybe your cat just knows it looks cute and that it makes them even harder to resist.

Bare belly

This is one of the most adorable ways for a cat to sleep, where it is on its back with all four paws in the air. It might not seem comfortable and it even looks a little silly, but it is the ultimate display of trust. The tummy is a cat's most vulnerable area, and a spot it would naturally try to hide from predators. When your cat sleeps this way, it is telling you it feels safe in your home and in your company. Try to resist the urge to rub its belly. That would be an insult after it has shown you that in no uncertain terms it trusts you, and it might leave your cat feeling annoyed or worse – see it as an invitation to scratch or bite you.

Cuddle buddies

Cats that are friendly with other cats in your home can often be found cuddling each other. Sometimes they will begin the ritual by cleaning each other before settling down for a nap. This type of napping or sleeping is a bonding ritual, but don't expect them to always sleep with their paws around each other. Cats, like people, need their own space from time to time. However, it is adorable to see two or more cats in a fur pile of love.

If your cat is an only feline, it may decide to cuddle with you instead. You might find your cat sleeping between your legs or pressed up against your back at night. It might even sleep on you or above your head. If you are taking a nap in the easy chair, a cuddle cat will often nap in your lap.

Zonking out on your clothes or shoes

Some cats love the smell of dirty clothes and will pick that gross place to catch 40 winks. Or you might find your cat sleeping on top of a pair of stinky shoes. As fastidious as cats are, some just cannot resist the smell of smelly things. What it is about the stinkiness that makes a cat want to sleep on it is anybody's guess. It just may be your cat's way of telling you it loves you, no matter what the smell.

Of course, your cat might also sleep on your clean clothes – the ones you have laid out and are about to wear. It might seem odd if those clothes are lying on your bed where there is ample other room to catch a nap. The fact that it chooses your nice clean outfit to snooze on instead of the rest of your bed may be indicative of just another way for your cat to feel closer to you. Besides, there isn't a feline owner anywhere who leaves the house without wearing a few cat hairs.

Sitting Like a Thanksgiving Turkey and Other Funny Cat Positions

You have probably seen your cat sitting on the floor with its legs tucked under it, making its body look like a turkey. No one knows why cats sit this way, but it could be a non aggressive or relaxed position, or a cat might feel more secure with its legs tucked under it.

Another common cat position is when a cat is on the prowl, about to "attack" its toy or even you. In this position, a cat's body is low to the ground and its eyes are totally focused on the object of its hunt. A tell tale sign that your cat is about to pounce is when it wiggles its butt. For your cat, this is serious play. For you, it is fun to watch.

When your cat wants you or another cat to play with it, it might roll back and forth on its back while reaching out to you or the other feline with its front paws. By showing its tummy, it is displaying a non aggressive message that it is ready to engage in some playful interaction.

Boxes, Bags and Other Non Cat Toys

Many a cat owner has spent a ton of money on cat toys, only to be frustrated by the discovery that their cat prefers the toy's packaging over the toy. In fact, cats have the ability to make a game out of just about any kind of household item. Buy a few cat toys from the pet store, if you wish, but don't be disappointed if your cat turns its back on those gifts you have lovingly chosen and prefers to make a toy out of items you have or use around your home.

Boxes and bags are two good examples. Cats are instinctively attracted to boxes and bags, or any type of container that they can hide in. Part of the appeal is the secure feeling they get when they are "boxed in." They also like to be incognito, away from our watching eyes. If you want entertainment, place an empty box or large paper bag in the middle of the floor. It will be hard for your cat to resist.

Laundry baskets are also containers that a cat loves to hide in. Nothing is more infuriating than doing a load of laundry, only to come back later and find your cat sleeping on the clean clothes. Cats also are able to squeeze into small spaces, so finding your feline in a decorative basket with only its head sticking out can be a hilarious sight. Try not to laugh, however, because cats are very sensitive about being made fun of. It may also be difficult to resist the urge to snap a picture of your kitty in this funny position. Just be prepared for your cat to give you the cold shoulder after you do. Also, make sure you do not leave plastic bags or bags with handles lying around and that you close cabinet doors that contain household cleaners that could be toxic to your cat. Its curiosity and love for small spaces can sometimes be a dangerous combination.

Some cats have one favorite toy. Others quickly lose interest in the latest gadget and move on to the next toy. Rotating toys can be one way to keep your kitty stimulated. So is choosing toys that mimic what a cat likes to naturally do – bat things around, hunt and pounce. You can also make your cat toys out of materials you have lying around.

For example, cats love to chase string and bat around items tied to ends of strings. There is no need to pay for a fancy pole and string toy when you can simply tie a thick string or rope on a door handle and tie a toy mouse on the other end, or tie a string or rope on a pole and run, dragging it behind while your cat chases it. Let your cat catch it everyone once in a while so that it feels it has caught its "prey."

Another easy and affordable toy is to take an empty pill bottle and put two jingle balls in it that you can purchase at any craft store. Put the lid on and watch your cat bat the jingling ball around. You can also use bean bag beans, dehydrated beans, or uncooked popcorn, or anything that makes a rattling sound that will make your cat want to bat it and chase it around.

A cat's natural instinct is to chase, so the simple act of balling up a piece of paper and throwing it at your cat is another cost-free game you can play with it. Some cats are known to like sticky notes, perhaps because of the paper's small size when wadded up. Cats have even been known to play a form of fetch where they chase after the sticky note and bring it back.

Toilet paper rolls are often a favorite toy for some cats. The round shape rolls easily across the floor, and the long tube makes it easy to bat around. Other cats like the round ring that is pulled off a milk container. It bounces and is easy for a cat to carry around in its mouth.

Some cats enjoy playing with catnip. Its pungent smell is appealing and when eaten can put a cat into a kind of trance or high. Other cats love to roll around in it. Some cats like to do both. You can make an affordable catnip toy by stuffing some of the plant into an old sock and typing up the end.

Hair bands are also a favorite toy of some cats, but this could be a dangerous toy. Cats may chew and swallow a hair band, which can obstruct the intestinal tract. Also, avoid letting your cat play with a ball of yarn, despite its reputation as a great cat toy. Yarn can cause intestinal obstruction, as can strings, rubber bands and ribbons left lying around. When it comes to bags, don't leave plastic ones or ones with handles lying around. Both can cause strangulation, and plastic bags can also cause suffocation. Play it safe and always supervise what your cat is playing with or chewing on to prevent an emergency trip to the vet.

Alarm Clock Cats

Contrary to popular belief, cats are not nocturnal. Nocturnal would mean they were up all night, when in fact they do sleep at night; they just don't sleep as long as people do. What cats are is *crepuscular*, which means their most active times are dawn and dusk, similar to the hunting times of their wild ancestors.

But a cat can also quickly adapt to its owner's sleeping and waking schedule because cats have the uncanny ability to synchronize their body clocks to our alarm clocks and personal habits. If you get up at the same time each day and immediately feed your kitty, it will soon catch on that the buzzing sound of your alarm or your own ability to awaken at a certain time translates into feeding time. If your cat starts pestering you to wake up and you comply, it will also quickly learn that pestering you earns it the award of eating. This is what you call owner training.

Once your cat has trained you to get up upon demand, it is futile to yell at your cat to knock it off. You have already taught your cat that its insistence will be rewarded. Cowering under the covers will only result in your cat being more determined than ever to get under there with you and bug you, or do annoying antics such as touching its paws to your face, getting a whisker up your nose, pouncing on you or kneading you, or biting exposed feet and hands, until you give in and get up.

Some cats are clever enough to learn which button turns on your alarm clock. Others push items off of your dresser so that they crash to the floor, scratch on the wood of the bed, put a paw under the door and rattle it, meow loudly, or do whatever noisy activities that will result in an awakened response from their owners.

Every time you relent and get up, you reinforce your cat's demanding behavior. But there are ways you can gain the upper hand with your alarm clock feline. Try putting light blocking curtains on the windows so that your bedroom is completely dark. Even though your cat's internal clock won't be fooled, this might keep your cat from thinking it is morning and time to get up – at least for a little while longer.

Also, feed your cat an hour or two later than when you arise, rather than the second you get up. This way, your cat won't associate you getting out of bed with feeding time. Even if your cat bugs you, wait until later to feed it its first meal. This will also allow you to feed it its second meal later in the evening, which should keep your kitty satisfied throughout the night.

Be sure to play with your cat a few times a day in order to tire it out. Make one of the playtimes right before you go to bed, to use up your cat's excess energy. This should lead to your feline sleeping longer during the night.

Also, think about getting a kitty friend for your cat. This will keep your cat from getting lonely when you are away, but will also keep it entertained while you are sleeping. If both cats bug you during the night or in the morning, consider sleeping with your door closed. Of course, many cats figure out how to rattle a bedroom door so that the noise will wake you up.

Whatever you do, don't give in and feed your cat if it pesters you in the early morning. Dawn is a natural feeding time in accordance with your cat's wild instincts, but that doesn't mean you have to comply. If you do get up, you will reinforce the behavior and the next thing you know, your cat will start waking you earlier and earlier in the morning.

The hardest part will be sticking to a feeding schedule. Cats like to break the rules if it means getting rewarded, in this case getting fed. It may take a while for your cat to catch on to your refusal to be trained to wake up and feed it when it wants you to, especially if you are trying to break an already established bad habit of feeding your cat on demand. But your persistence will pay off in the form of getting your much needed sleep.

One easy thing to remember is that there are four stages to a cat's day that are inherited from its wild ancestors: hunting, feeding, grooming and sleep. If you play with your cat before bed and then give it a snack (or make that its second meal of the day), it will then naturally groom since all cats groom after eating, another carry over from its wild ancestors who cleaned after eating to remove the scent of its prey in order not to attract a predator. After a cat grooms, it always takes a nap or goes to sleep. Doing this series at bedtime should keep both you and your cat happy – you with a night of undisturbed sleep, and your cat with stimulating activity followed by a tasty treat.

Also, remember that if you are gone all day, your cat wants your attention when you come home. If you walk in the door, feed it and then ignore it, then go off to bed, your kitty will find a way to get your attention, even if that means waking you early. Be sure to spend time with your cat before heading off to bed. Also, bring out toys that are different from the ones your cat plays with during the day. This should keep your cat occupied during its waking times at night and in the morning.

In addition, if you do not want your cat to sleep in your bedroom, make sure it sleeps in a room or area of the house it feels comfortable in or wants to sleep in. One way to do this is to create a kitty bed that has your scent on it – such as a pile of your clothes or some of your old shirts that you do not mind getting cat hair on. You can also train your kitty to use a cat perch or cat bed by using a clicker or saying "bedtime," patting the bed, and when it lies in it, giving it a treat. Leave a few favorite toys near the bed, so that your cat might play when it awakens during the night. And whatever you do, don't get up if your cat meows outside your bedroom door or you will reinforce this behavior.

Finally, remember that your cat's morning antics go beyond just wanting to be fed. Cats are safer when kept indoors but this can also eliminate the mental and physical stimulation a cat gets when it is allowed to roam the great outdoors. Take the time to spend time with your cat, especially if you are at work all day. Brush it, play with it, and talk to your cat. The attention may be all your feline needs to keep it from waking you up, and it will reduce boredom that can lead to depression.

Toilet Paper Cats

One of the funniest sights is seeing a cat claw at a roll of toilet paper in its holder, causing the paper to be shredded and completely unroll in the process. This, of course, can also be infuriating, not to mention, messy. However, this is another great opportunity to use a clicker or clap your hands loudly while saying, "no," in order to break your cat of this habit – provided, of course, you can catch your cat in the act and not after the fact, when your bathroom has been turned into a snowy display of hundreds of pieces of toilet paper.

Why so many cats find a toilet roll on a holder fascinating is anybody's guess. Perhaps it is the rapid-fire unrolling that some cats find enjoyable, or the appealing texture of the paper that makes clawing it hard to resist. Sometimes this is the result of a lack of enough scratching posts in your home, so your cat quickly learns that toilet paper can be a perfect replacement when the urge to scratch kicks in.

Whatever the case, if this is a behavior your cat loves to indulge in, you might want to nip it in the bud – unless, of course, you do not mind going through roll after wasted roll. One way to do this is to squeeze the roll prior to placing it in the holder, so that the inside cardboard doesn't roll easily. There are also child-proof toilet rollers that can prevent your cat from having access to the toilet paper or that only allow one or two sheets of paper to be released at a time.

Keep in mind that in addition to unrolling the toilet paper, many cats find the bathroom in general to be fascinating and fun. For example, some felines like to lick the condensation droplets that can build up on a toilet tank when the weather is warm. Batting items off the bathroom counter is another amusing activity that some cats find pleasurable.

Cats often enjoy watching us bathe or shower, although no one knows why. Perhaps they are curious about our need to immerse ourselves in water or that we have no fur and they find our nakedness puzzling. Some felines will sit on their owners' laps while they use the toilet. Others will use their litter boxes at the same time their people are using the toilet, as if there is some kind of camaraderie in eliminating at the same time. Cats have also been known to stare at their humans while their people relieve themselves.

Some cats find sinks to be the perfect place to take a nap. The size and shape seem designed for a cat, and some felines might find the porcelain to be cooling in warm weather. Other cats like to drink from the faucet because they find the fresh, cold water more appealing than the water sitting around in their bowls.

Your cat could be doing these fun activities – at least fun for your cat – because it is bored. Try to create a fun household environment filled with stimulating toys, and make sure you take the time to play with your cat at least twice a day. If your cat still insists on using your bathroom as a playground and this is unacceptable to you, keep the bathroom door closed – unless, of course, that is where you keep the litter box!

The Kitty Art of Opening Doors

Cats are very observant animals and learn from watching people and pets around them. Some cats can actually learn how to turn a door handle or open a door simply from observing their owners do it.

Some cats learn how to turn door handles, while others can undo a latch. Some do it by leaping into the air until their paws can grab the door handle or by getting on top of a nearby object that is at the door handle's height. This might require persistence, even if it takes several tries. But one thing is for sure – there is no stopping a cat that is determined to go through a door to a room or the outdoors if that is what it has set its mind to.

Cats have been known to get into pantries where they know the food or treats are kept. Some felines are able to open drawers and rummage around, flicking out items they want on to the floor. The fact is, a cat learns by self-motivation and is adept at learning anything that benefits its own self-interest. If the experience is bad, a cat will not repeat it. But if the experience is beneficial, such as opening a door or drawer that leads to or contains what it wants, a cat will repeat the experience.

Of course, having your cat open a door is not always a good thing, especially if that door leads to the outside or a room or cabinet that contains items that are harmful to your kitty. You can prevent this from happening by putting a deadbolt lock on the door or child protector locks on cabinets and drawers. If your cat has the habit of running out your front or back door when it is opened, make it an unpleasant experience by putting double stick tape on the floor in front of the door. If your cat is opening the door by getting up on something that is the same height as the doorknob, remove that furniture or item far enough away so that your cat isn't able to reach the knob or latch.

If you allow your cat to go outside, you might want to install a cat door. But keep in mind that cat doors are also invitations to raccoons and other critters that might be able to gain entry into your house, putting you, your family and your pets at risk.

The Need to be Near Us

Cats are independent and solitary by nature, but that doesn't mean they don't enjoy our company. They are not pack animals, but most do enjoy socializing with us and being part of the family.

You may notice that your cat sits near you or hangs out wherever you are in your home. Take this as a compliment in that your cat wants to be near you. Your cat might sit on your lap or on the couch next to you. Or it might sit quietly across the room, enjoying your company.

Your cat might lean against you, wanting to make physical contact. It might sit on your desk or even on your computer keyboard, or on the top of the back of your chair. Felines have a reputation of being distant and aloof, but this typical behavior that is experienced by many cat owners suggests otherwise. Cats in fact enjoy being with us, whether from a distance or right smack up beside us. The fact is, your cat could choose to sleep or hang out somewhere else in your home that might be more comfortable – and maybe sometimes it does. But when it chooses instead to be near you, it is expressing its deep affection for you.

Kneading us

Perhaps the sweetest display of affection is when your cat kneads you. This is a replay of how it kneaded its mother when it was a kitten in order to get her to express her milk. When your cat kneads you, sometimes called "making biscuits," it is telling you it trusts you and loves you. Often, cats will alternate their paws, first one and then the other. Your cat may do this when you are petting it, or it may spontaneously do this on its own. Not all cats knead their owners. If yours does, it is just one of many ways of displaying its trust and fondness for you. It may be a little uncomfortable, but take it as a compliment and as a sign of adoration.

Going Along For the Ride –
Talking Down Your Anxious Cat

There will come a time when you will need to take your cat for a ride in the car. It may be for a vet visit, or because you are moving, or because you are going on vacation, or you need to take your cat away from your home for some reason. While there are cats who do not mind traveling in cars, most find it to be a frightening experience. They don't like the noises from the car and other vehicles on the road, or the quick moving visuals whipping by while you are driving. Simply put, cats don't take to car rides the way many dogs do, but there are ways you can help to alleviate the stress most cats feel when riding in cars.

Keep Your Cat Contained

Whenever you travel with your cat, *always* use a cat carrier. A carrier not only keeps your kitty safe, it keeps you safe as well.

Cats like the feeling of being in small, contained places, so a cat carrier can go a long way in alleviating the stress your feline feels when having to travel in your car.

In addition, a carrier prevents your cat from wandering around your car while you are driving, especially if your kitty is anxious about riding in your car. If your cat is allowed to roam, it will try to seek out a small, private space. That could be under your brake, gas pedal or your foot, or under a car seat. This can be distracting and dangerous, especially if your cat winds up under one of the pedals. Your cat might also leap onto the dashboard or on to you, which could lead to an accident. A carrier allows you to concentrate on driving and not on your cat, which keeps you both safe in your travels.

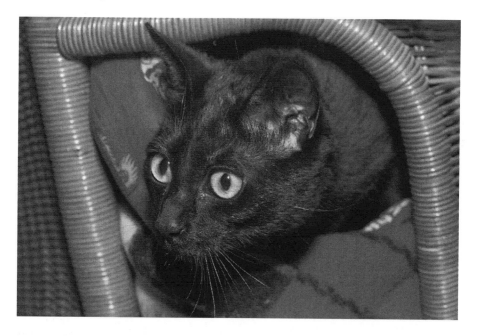

When purchasing a carrier, make sure it is one that is large enough for your cat to turn around, and that it is well ventilated. Look for one that is sturdy with a strong and secure latch that will stay closed. If your cat is large, you might want to get a carrier that has wheels on it or pull it on a wheeler so that you do not injure yourself when carrying it. Be sure to put your cat in it before you leave the house, rather than attempt to do this inside your car. You might want to put a soft towel or blanket or a t-shirt with your smell on it inside so that your cat feels more comfortable. Don't forget to bring bowls for food and water, as well as a disposable litter box, if you plan on taking your feline on a long journey.

Also, be sure to latch a seatbelt around that carrier, if possible, in order to prevent the carrier from going airborne if you get involved in an accident. You can also purchase carriers that have clips that attach to seatbelts, which helps to prevent the carrier from slipping out of the seatbelt.

If your cat isn't used to riding in a carrier or hates the experience, try to get it used to the ordeal beforehand. Start by leaving the carrier out on your floor the day or a few days prior to your trip, move or vet visit. Leave the door open to entice your cat to go inside and try it out. Most cats can't resist going into a small enclosed area. Then on the day it has to ride in the carrier, it might go right inside. If it doesn't, then slip your cat in backwards. Have someone else hold the carrier on its end and carefully drop your cat in, tail first.

Make sure that your cat wears a collar with its identification tag on it every time it travels in your car. The ID tag should have your cell phone number on it or the number of the chip company that knows how to get in touch with you should, tragically, your cat escape during your trip or car ride. If your cat hasn't been microchipped, definitely consider doing this before you take your cat for a car ride. It could mean the difference between you getting your cat back or not should it get loose. Also, consider getting a harness and leash, if you need to stop along the way to allow your cat to use the litter box. This will keep your cat secure and prevent it from running off.

Ready, Set, Go

Once your cat is in its carrier and you are ready to set off on your destination, you can keep it calm by letting it know you are near-by and there for your cat. One way to do this is to place the carrier so that you are able to make eye contact with your cat. This doesn't mean taking your eyes off the road by turning around, but rather, glancing at your cat in the rearview mirror. Cats have the uncanny ability of knowing to look at the mirror in order to see your eyes. Just knowing that you are visually there can go a long way in calming your cat.

Talking softly and repeating its name here and there will also help to alleviate your cat's anxieties. So will playing soothing music that can help it relax, and bringing along its favorite toys to put in the carrier, provided that there is room. Singing to your cat is another option, especially if you sing its name in the song. For some reason, "Lullabye" is a song that works well in getting your cat to take a nap, maybe for the same unknown reason it works with human babies.

You can also spray your cat's carrier with a natural pheromone spray about 15 minutes prior to leaving. The pheromones have a calming effect that some owners find beneficial. In addition, you can get a prescription for a sedative for your cat from your veterinarian if you have to travel long distance, but these types of medicines often have the opposite intended effect and can make your cat actually feel worse.

Finally, it should go without saying that you should never, ever leave your cat unattended in your car. Not only will this make your feline feel even more anxious, but the inside temperature of your car could rise and cause serious health issues for your cat – and even death. In addition, someone could steal your cat while you are away, even if you are only gone a few minutes. If you must leave your vehicle, take your cat in the carrier with you.

Cats on the Move

There may come a time when you decide to move, and you will need to make the transition as easy as possible for your cat. Cats are very sensitive to any changes in their environment, so moving can be a stressful experience for a cat.

To lessen the trauma of relocating that may be felt by your cat, you should begin by preparing your cat beforehand. For example, bring out the cat carrier a week before you move and allow your cat to sniff it and even go inside it. Leave the carrier's door open the entire time, and put a favorite blanket or one of your shirts with your scent on it inside. When moving day comes, your cat may then be less resistant to getting in the carrier.

If you are packing boxes, allow your cat to sniff and rub on them and even go inside them. But be sure to double check where your cat is before you tape any boxes shut. You don't want your cat to accidentally get trapped inside, which could be traumatic and even deadly.

Also, keep a very close eye on your cat when packing for the move. Cats can get out when the door is open while loading the moving truck. Cats also hate their domain being dismantled, and may decide to hide rather than be around for the disruption. Some cats have been known to run away from the stress of moving day. You might want to have someone watch your cat during the process of packing and moving. If that is not possible, then put your cat in a secure room, away from the comings and goings, and move your cat *last*. Put a note on the door to remind your movers or anyone who is helping with the move not to open the door. Whether you are moving long distance, across town, or just down the street, know where your cat is at all times!

In addition, make sure your cat is up-to-date on vaccines, especially if you are moving out of the country. Also, get its veterinarian records in order and within easy reach, in case you need them on your moving journey. Have your cat wear its collar with its identification and rabies tags attached when making your move. And if your cat isn't microchipped, consider getting it done. If for some unforeseen reason, your cat gets lost during your move, the microchip can help make sure your kitty is returned to you. If your cat is already chipped, contact the microchip company to confirm that it has your current cell phone number and any other pertinent information, such as the name and phone number of your veterinarian or a close relative or friend, and your new address.

If your cat doesn't travel well, talk to your veterinarian about possibly getting a sedative or an all natural stress-relieving alternative to give your kitty for the trip. If your move is long distance and you are traveling by car, do your research beforehand in order to find pet-friendly hotels where you and your cat can stay on the way. Bring along a disposable litter box, as well as your cat's food and water bowls.

If you are flying to your new home, be sure that your cat carrier has enough room for your cat to move around while still meeting your airline's size and weight requirements. You might be able to bring your cat into the plane's cabin if it can fit under your seat. If not, then research the conditions of where your cat will be kept underneath the plane. You want to verify that it will be heated or at least a comfortable temperature, and that the air pressure will be pet safe. Also investigate your airline's reputation on keeping pets safe *before* booking your flight. There have been cases where pets have gotten out of their carriers and gotten lost, harmed or even died, or who never make their connecting flights and are lost along the way. A better solution might be to pay to have your cat transported by one of the many pet transport van or truck companies that will drive your cat to your new destination for a fee.

Even if you are only moving down the street or across town, secure your cat in its carrier. An accident can happen anywhere, and you want to make sure you keep your cat safe. You also want to prevent your cat who is probably stressed by all of the upheaval of packing from getting under the gas pedal or brake or hiding under the seat. Talk to your cat and use its name often on the drive. Your cat will find your voice comforting. You can also play soothing music and position the carrier so that your cat is able to make eye contact with you.

When you get to your new destination, again put your cat in a secure room while you or the movers unpack your belongings. Put a blanket with your scent on it in the room with your cat, along with its food and water bowls, and even toys your cat knows or that are its favorites. Include a scratching post so that your cat can begin to make its mark in your new home. Your cat should begin to relax with all of the familiar items around it. Don't forget to place a note on the door to remind everyone who is coming and going that your cat is in the room and therefore they should not open the door.

Once the movers are gone and all of your furniture and boxes are in your new place, let your cat out of the room. Allow your kitty to explore your new home and take in all the new scents. However, your cat might prefer to stay in the room and could take a day or two before feeling confident enough to check out the rest of your new home. Let your feline set the pace of when it wants to begin exploring.

Take time to play with your cat once you are in your new place. You may be distracted by all of the unpacking and other changes in your life, but playtime can calm your cat, alleviate stress, and make it feel more confident about being in a new environment. Also, keep its schedule as normal as possible. Stick to the same eating times and try to go to bed at your usual hour. Don't forget to show your cat the new location of the litter box. It might be tempting to buy a new one, but you might want to start off by using the box its familiar with. Also, invite your cat to come to bed with you, especially if that is your usual ritual. Feeling you sleeping next to it can be comforting to your cat.

It can take a cat up to a month to feel comfortable in its new surroundings. Cats need this amount of time to reset their internal honing abilities, which is why it is not unusual for indoor/outdoor cats to return to their old neighborhoods after their owners move. If your cat is allowed to go outside, it is very important to keep it indoors when you first move into your new place so that it doesn't wander off in search of your old home. Wait until your home seems familiar to your cat and it is no longer stressed, before you allow it to go outside. This might also be a good time to make your cat an inside-only cat, since going outside presents dangerous conditions for all cats.

Your cat might also try to hide in small places in your new house in order to feel secure. Make sure to close off any small space that could pose a danger, such as a fireplace with a chimney, closets, or under furniture such as a reclining chair that can crush a cat that is hiding underneath it. You might want to create a special corner with a cat bed or blanket but give your cat its space until it adjusts to your new home.

If you must go to work shortly after you move and your cat will be left alone during the day, keep a radio or a TV on. The noise and voices will be comforting. Allow your cat the run of your home so that it can spend the first few days checking out the place. This will help pass the time until you return at the end of the day. When you do get home, be sure to spend the first ten or 15 minutes with your cat in order to alleviate any fears it has about being left alone in an unfamiliar environment. Remember, the move might be exciting for you but your cat won't share your enthusiasm. How you handle the ordeal will determine how well your feline makes the transition. Your cat will pick up on your mood, so by staying upbeat and positive, you can help your kitty to view the whole moving situation as a curious adventure.

First Impressions –
How to Introduce Your Cat
to a New Member
of the Family

amilies change, people remarry, divorce and have babies. These constant fluctuations may be a natural part of life's flow for you, but to your cat, any changes to your family dynamics translate to chaos and stress.

This is especially true when you bring home a new baby or marry. Your cat is used to being the center of your attention, your "baby" if you will, so a new member of your family that now commands most of your attention could stir up feline feelings of hurt, jealousy and rejection.

Baby on Board

Some people see a new baby on the way as a necessity to get rid of their cat. Many cats are abandoned at shelters each year because well meaning family and friends – and even doctors – convince parents-to-be that it is dangerous to have a cat around a new baby. Others are left to fend for themselves outside, which can be especially traumatic for a once inside cat. Both scenarios are unnecessary but you do need to take some precautions. Never leave your newborn baby alone with your cat and don't allow your cat to sleep with the baby since, in an effort to cuddle up to your newborn, a cat might unintentionally sit on the baby, making breathing difficult for your newborn.

You can make the transition of having a new baby in the home easier for your cat by planning ahead. First begin by allowing your cat to sniff any new baby furniture you have set up and to explore the baby's room *prior* to the baby's birth. Let your cat smell new blankets and clothes, and even talk to your cat about the new baby. Also, sprinkle baby powder or spread baby lotion on you, so that your kitty gets used to the smell.

In addition, you might want to purchase one of those dolls that cry or play recordings of babies crying and making baby noises, so that your cat gets accustomed to the sounds. Also, carry around a baby doll, so that your feline gets used to the idea of you having a baby in your arms. If you know what you are naming your baby, say its name often to your cat prior to the birth. This will help your feline connect the name to the baby once it is brought home.

When you finally bring the new baby home, allow your cat to sniff its smell, rather than shooing your cat away. Let your cat sit next to you when you feed and hold the baby, so that your feline feels part of the process. Also, limit scolding, ignoring or isolating your cat, or it will feel stressed and rejected and may resent the baby. This isn't always easy since having a new baby can be overwhelming and take up a lot of your time, but it is important that you still give some time and attention to your kitty each day.

Another good idea is to discourage your cat from jumping into the baby crib or on the changing table. Do this *before* you bring the baby home by putting double stick tape in the crib or on the table, or by purchasing a crib cover. This way, by the time your newborn arrives, your cat will no longer be interested in checking out the crib or lounging on the changing table. If you decide that your baby's room is off limits for your cat, consider getting a baby gate. A gate is better than just closing the door – which can always intrigue a cat and make it determined to open it to get inside – because it allows your cat to still see and hear what is going on in the baby's room. If your cat does get in the baby's room, remove it gently but don't scold it. You don't want to do anything that makes your cat associate your new baby with negativity.

Also, try to keep a consistent schedule with your cat in regards to its regular feeding times. This is not an easy feat, since having a new baby is time consuming, but it will keep your cat happy and stress free. Cats are consistent animals and hate anything that disrupts their lives and routine. It only takes a minute to feed your cat, which will keep it content and less concerned about the new baby. Don't forget to clean the litter box regularly and take time each day to give your feline attention. By keeping your cat's routine flowing as usual, you will prevent it from acting out in negative ways, such as eliminating outside the box. The last thing you need when you have a new baby is to have to deal with behavioral problems from your cat. You do not need the stress and neither does your kitty.

You may have frequent visits from family and friends who want to come and see your new baby. During these times, keep your cat in a quiet room, away from the comings and goings of your guests. Don't forget to place its food, water and litter box in the room, along with a favorite toy or blanket. This quiet retreat can prevent your feline from feeling nervous and stressed from all the noise and excitement.

Finally, encourage a good relationship between your cat and your baby by praising your kitty when it behaves around your baby. Make sure to supervise the time spent between them, especially as your baby gets bigger and wants to pet your cat. Toddlers can be rough with animals and may pet your cat too hard or pull its tail. You don't want your cat to retaliate by scratching or biting your baby, or for it to be in fear of your child. You might also want to place kitty perches out of reach of your toddler's hands, so that your cat can escape should it feel the need. In addition, move the litter box to a quiet, private area that is inaccessible to your child but easy to get to for your cat.

Try to remember that in its mind it was here first, so don't let your cat feel as if it has been replaced. A few minutes of your time and a little preparation beforehand can make a world of difference in your cat's feelings towards your baby and in their future relationship together.

Changing Family Dynamics

You can expect your family dynamics to change over time, but that doesn't mean it will be easy for your cat. A new boyfriend or girlfriend, marriage, or the move-in of relative or friend can be a stressful change to your feline's environment. Cats are territorial and yours might view the new addition as a threat. Don't try to force the new person on your cat. The relationship has to evolve gradually.

Try not to make changes in your cat's routine that could be viewed as upsetting or confusing. For example, if your cat is used to sleeping on your bed or in a certain room, and is suddenly kicked off or out, this could be viewed as rejection by your kitty, which in turn may lead to behavioral problems. If at all possible, include your cat in the new threesome on your bed, or if a guest is now using the room your cat once claimed as its own, see if your guest is willing to share the space.

It should be noted that you cannot rush the acceptance of a new spouse or new member of the family. A cat has to make up its own mind. If at all possible, start by having your new housemate bring some clothes over or something with his or her scent on it, so that your cat can get used to the new smells *before* this person moves in. You can also take a piece of clothing and rub your cat's scent on it. Then have your new family member or guest bring the item in to your home with its own belongings. If neither of these scenarios is possible – for example, say your new houseguest is moving in from far away – then place an item with your cat's smell on it in with the new family member's stuff after he or she has arrived. This will send a message to your cat that this person is a member of your clan.

Next, have your new mate or guest prepare your cat's food or give it some treats. If your cat won't take the food or treat directly from your new person, then at least let it view the preparation or treats from a distance so that it knows it came from your new spouse or house member. Nothing spells love more to a feline than food, and your cat will start associating tasty good things with the new person on the scene.

Playing with your cat is a great way to gain acceptance of your new significant other or housemate because it allows your cat to build trust with that person. Have this person interact with your kitty for a few minutes each day. Cats cannot resist a good game of play, and this can help yours view the new person as fun rather than as a threat. If your cat isn't willing at first to play with him or her, then start by playing with your cat yourself while this person sits on the sidelines. Once your cat has relaxed and is enjoying itself, hand off the toy to this other person. Eventually, your feline might allow your guest to initiate the play session.

Finally, make sure your cat has a room or place to retreat to if need be. If you don't have an extra room, then at least give your cat a perch where it can avoid interacting with your new family member. Instruct your spouse or guest to leave your cat alone whenever it is in its perch or safe area. Also, make sure its litter box is in a private area not trafficked by this person.

If your cat gradually walks over to your new family member, allow it to sniff without being touched. Don't rush the interaction; let it be on your cat's terms. It might take a while for your cat to warm up to the new person in your life, so try to make the transition as easy and stress-free as possible.

Adding a New Pet to the Fold

Bringing a new cat or dog or any new pet into home can be especially stressful to your cat, even if it has previously lived with other cats and dogs. For your resident cat, a newcomer presents a disruption and a possible threat, and must be handled carefully in order to ensure success.

Creating a Clowder

If you are adopting a cat to keep your current feline company, try to choose one that has previously lived with other cats. If your cat is young or middle-aged, you might want to consider a kitten so that your cat is the alpha cat, if you will. But if your cat is old, a kitten might present too much stressful energy. In fact, you should reconsider adopting *any* cat if you own an elderly cat that is used to living on its own.

When adopting a second cat, choose one that is a different size and age of your current kitty. This can avoid any fighting that can occur between cats of the same size and age group. Often, cats of the opposite sex get along best, but this is not always the case. Like people, cats just "click" with some cats and not with others. Many bonds have been formed between same sex cats that can often be found playing, grooming and sleeping together. Rather than base your choices on whether a new cat is the same sex or opposite sex, try to find a new cat that is friendly and has a similar temperament and energy level as your current feline.

It is also important to consider your cat's situation, in addition to its temperament. If you spend hours at work or travel a lot, a fellow feline friend could be just what your cat needs in order to prevent loneliness and boredom. But if you have recently moved or your cat has lost a beloved cat friend or favorite dog, or is ill or has some other issue or crisis going on, this is not the time to introduce a new cat. You want to make sure your cat is ready to meet a new member of the family.

When you have decided on your new cat, introduce it to your resident cat very carefully. Expect there to be some hissing and growling at first, although this might not be the case. You must give your primary cat time to adjust. Sometimes owners view the initial hissy fight as a sign that their cat will not accept the new feline. Although this can sometimes be the case since some cats are extremely territorial or there is an unresolveable personality conflict, often your primary cat's initial response is just a knee-jerk reaction to an unexpected new resident.

One of the best ways to introduce a new cat to an established one is to have someone who doesn't live in your home bring the new cat in. Make sure the newbie is in a carrier when this happens, so that your resident cat doesn't feel betrayed by you and neither cat feels threatened. Have a sanctuary room prepared for the new cat and place it in there. This will give it a space to retreat to until it gets used to your home and your resident cat.

Next, close the door and give your resident cat a treat. Play with it or feed it, in order to create a distraction. This may or may not work – chances are, your cat's entire focus is on the new cat behind the door. This is not unusual and is actually a good thing because it will allow the two cats to "meet" without having a face-to-face confrontation. Your resident cat may sniff around the door or sit in front of it, or your cat and the new one may even play "paws" under the door. Allow your cat plenty of time to get used to the idea that there is another cat behind the door. This might take anywhere from one day to one week, but keep your new feline in the sanctuary room until your resident cat seems comfortable that there is a new cat on the scene.

Feed and visit the new cat only at those times when your primary cat is eating, sleeping or away from the door. If your resident cat sees you going into the room, it might get upset about the attention you are paying the newbie. Once it seems calm about the other cat, that is, you see it sitting calmly in front of the door, then take two socks and rub one on your primary cat, and bring it into the room. Take the other sock and rub it on the new feline and bring that out to your resident cat. This allows both cats to get used to each other's scent before their face-to-face meeting.

If your resident cat reacts badly to the sock, do not reprimand it. You do not want it to associate anything negative, such as a scolding, with the new feline. Instead, engage your cat in play and ignore its reaction to the sock. Once it stops reacting to the sock over time, then put your resident cat in another room. This is when it is time to bring out the new kitty and allow it to investigate your home and leave its scent throughout as it rubs on furniture, walls and other objects.

If by this time, your resident cat has remained calm, it is time for the two cats to meet. Start by opening the door to your new cat's sanctuary room and feed the two cats in sight of each other but not together. Do this a little each day, but keep the group sessions short. Gradually, you can inch their cat bowls closer to each other. If either cat seems stressed out or aggressive, keep a baby gate on the door. This way they can eat within each other's sight, without feeling territorial. Be sure to stand between them during these feeding times and never leave them alone together. If the cats are staring at each other, use a clicker and give a treat to the cat who looks away first.

As the two cats get used to sharing your home, continue to allow the new cat access to the sanctuary room. This will give it a safe refuge to go to should it feel threatened or stressed by your other cat. Set up litter boxes for each cat in different locations. This insures harmony in that neither cat feels it has to compete for the litter box, especially if either becomes territorial about a certain area of your home.

It may take some time for your cats to become used to living with each other. There may continue to be some tense moments as each learns to negotiate and claim its own personal space. Also, be sure to invest in a cat perch, so that if one cat needs to get away from the other, it has a high up place to go. Take time to play with the cats together, such as swinging a string at one and then the other, or tossing a ball to one and then to the other. The red light chaser toy is a good one, but stop the game if in the excitement one or both cats get aggressive.

Over time, your cats may become close friends, or just roommates – or they may never really like each other. Use a clicker to diffuse any acts of aggression and give a treat to them when they comply. Eventually, at the very least, they should get used to living under the same roof. The key to harmony is to make sure each has its own space if need be and that you pay each an equal amount of attention.

Adding a dog to the mix

If you are adopting a dog, pick one who likes cats or, better yet, has lived with cats before. Choose a breed or mix that has a calm personality, rather than one that gets excited by smaller animals it views as prey. Even though our society has the idea that dogs and cats cannot get along, many dogs and cats actually form loving and lasting bonds. In fact, it is not unusual for a cat who cannot tolerate living with another cat to accept a dog roommate without question. Of course, cats and dogs communicate differently, so it will be up to you to intervene when necessary.

Once you have decided on a dog that seems like a good match for your cat, you will need to introduce them gradually. Remember, cats hate change – even one who has previously lived with a dog – so you want to make sure your cat and dog get off on the right paw.

Start by elevating your cat's food bowl *prior* to bringing the dog home, so that your cat gets used to eating out of range of the dog. This will prevent your dog from nibbling or eating your cat's food later, and will alleviate any tension between the two as a result. You might also want to feed them at different times in order to make mealtimes calmer for your kitty.

Also, place the litter boxes away from your dog's prying eyes but within easy access for your cat. Cats need their privacy when doing their business, so make sure your cat can go in peace. If need be, put a baby gate with a pet door in front of the room the litter box is in. If you feel the need to relocate the litter box, make the change gradually before your dog arrives.

In addition, make sure your cat has a room it can use as a safe retreat or a cat perch it can escape to, especially when your dog is new on the scene or if your cat doesn't come to enjoy its company. Train the new dog to stay out of this room or away from the perch.

When the first face-to-face meeting occurs, put your dog on a leash. Place your cat in another room with a baby gate so that the two can exchange smells. Sit outside the room with the dog and give it treats if it remains calm. Use a clicker to catch the dog's attention and then give it treats when it is focused on you instead of your cat. If you see your dog staring at your cat or making a movement in its direction, say the words, "Watch me!" while putting your finger on your nose. Whenever your dog obeys this command, praise it and give it a treat.

If your cat seems stressed by the presence of your dog, even though it is on the other side of the gate, close the door and keep your dog at a distance. Over the next several days, open the door for a few minutes at a time until you see that both the cat and dog seem relaxed in each other's company. Next, put your dog on a leash, take the gate down, and allow your cat to walk around your home. If your dog pulls on the leash, move it farther away from the cat. Eventually, your dog will learn that it is only allowed near your cat when it stops pulling on the leash. This will teach your dog that as long as it remains calm and relaxed and approaches your cat slowly, it will be rewarded with praises and treats.

When you leave your home, do not allow your cat and dog to have access to each other. Put them each in a separate room and make sure the doors are secure. Over time, the novelty of the cat should wear thin for your dog. Many dogs and cats live co-existing lives and become quite fond of each other. If this doesn't happen in your home and your dog continues to display aggressive behavior, then you have to consider that this is not a good dog and cat match. Contact a dog trainer who can work with your dog to see if the situation might improve. Safety should be your priority, and if your cat is the resident pet, its happiness should come first.

There's a Tiger
in Every Cat

wning a domestic cat is the closest that most of us will ever get to living alongside a wild cat. In fact, cats and their bigger cousins share many similar traits. Go to a zoo and witness a lion, tiger, puma, leopard, or some other big cat cleaning itself, stretching, playing, stalking, pouncing, kneading, or lying in the sun, and you will be viewing a larger copy of your own little tiger at home.

In fact, domesticated cats have the same anatomy, features and senses as big cats because all cats – domestic and wild – evolved from a single prehistoric ancestor. This is why it can be difficult for archeologists to tell whether ancient bones found at a site are those of a housecat or a similarly sized wild cat. As mentioned earlier in this book, the domestication of cats occurred later than dogs, horses and cattle, and not because we sought it out. As humans became farmers and left their hunter-gatherer lifestyle behind, we began to experience the threat to our food supplies of rodents. Cats saw the opportunity of a never ending meal, and invited themselves in to take care of the problem. Over time, humans and cats learned to co-exist, which somewhere along the line developed into a relationship of mutual affection.

Today, pet cats share comparable behaviors with wild felines, such as those gestures mentioned above, as well as scent marking either through rubbing or spraying and covering their feces. Diet is also similar since all cats, domestic and wild, need only one ingredient in their diet – meat – and can literally go blind and die without it. This is why vegetarians should never force their dietary choices on their felines. Cats, both wild and domesticated, are biologically made to ingest meat and only meat. Any carbohydrates that wild and domesticated cats get come from what their prey has eaten, or in the case of pet cats, vegetable carbs that are added to store bought food.

Night time vision is another trait that domesticated cats share with their wild cousins. Although no cat can see in total darkness, cats are able to see better than humans in low light levels. Cats only need one-sixth of the amount of light that humans need in order to make out shapes. This ability is shared by wild cats that do most of their hunting at night.

Even the act of kneading on you, where your cat presses down with one paw and then the other just as a kitten does to get its mother's milk, is a display of wild behavior. Wild cats do the same affectionate behavior with each other and also knead to pat down a bed of leaves or other materials before laying down for a nap.

Grooming after eating is a behavior your cat also shares with wild felines. You might think your cat does it because it loves to be clean, but the act runs deeper than that. It is an inherited wild trait of protection to remove any traces of its meal from its fur. In nature, wild cats don't want the scent of their eaten kill to alert any other potential prey, nor do they want to draw attention from predators. Observe your cat after it has eaten a meal. It will always groom itself afterwards. This is also almost *always* followed up by a nap in order to conserve its energy for the next "hunt" – just as its wild relatives do.

Taming the Wild Side

Some domesticated cats today act wilder than others, and many pedigreed cats are bred to specifically retain either wild genes or more laidback ones. If your cat is suddenly acting out in a wild form of aggression, however, lack of attention from you may be to blame. Your cat may have energy that needs to be spent, and will behave in destructive ways if it isn't allowed to or able to. If this is the case, spend time with your cat playing stalking and pouncing games. Your kitty will enjoy the attention while using up its excess energy.

The act of scratching is another form of wild behavior, similar to how big cats mark their territories. It is a scratch cats need to itch. Make sure to place scratching posts throughout your home in easy to get to locations, or your furniture or drapes may become your cat's target.

Another form of wild behavior is stalking and "hunting" at night or at dusk and dawn. These are the times that cats in the wild are the most active. If your cat is keeping you up at night with its jumping, running and pouncing, spend time playing with it during the day and then again right before you go to bed. You will help your feline use up untapped energy while taking care of its "wild" needs. Tire your cat out so that it spends the night sleeping rather than racing through your home.

If your cat is allowed to outside, do not be surprised if it brings you "gifts" of prey, such as dead mice, birds and insects. If your cat is an inside only cat, these gifts might be in the form of toy mice, bouncy balls and balled-up paper, or any unfortunate fly, cricket or insect that is unlucky enough to be trapped inside your home. Your feline is merely acting out its wild hunting desires and is bringing home a meal to the pride, in this case you or your family. No matter how many thousands of years of domestication have occurred, your cat still enjoys the wild practice of stalking, pouncing, and taking joy in the "hunt."

Testing the territorial boundaries

Sometimes your cat might surprise you by turning into an aggressive, territorial maniac. When this happens, it is important to find out why. Cats behave this way for a reason, and you need to figure out what has triggered the behavior.

Keep in mind that in the wild, being territorial and aggressive are means of survival. Territorial aggression can help a wild cat catch prey, mate, defend its pride, and keep its cubs alive. For pet cats, aggression serves other purposes, such as making sure another cat or dog doesn't eat its food or in letting you know that it is unhappy or isn't feeling well.

There are always warning signs leading up to an act of aggression. Your cat might let out a low growl, its skin might twitch and its tail may move back and forth, and there may even be a paw smack. When this happens, back off. Otherwise you could find yourself on the receiving end of a bite or scratch.

Like big cats, your pet cat might display sudden, unpredictable territorial behavior. This can occur when it sees another cat outside the window, or if you bring home a new pet. It is important to handle the situation carefully, as mentioned in Chapter 10, or your cat might act out its displeasure by eliminating outside the litter box or in other negative ways. If the problem is an outside cat, chase it away or make loud noises to discourage it from treading on your cat's territory. If the reason is because of a new pet, baby or person living in your home, then make sure your cat has space to call its own and that it receives a lot of attention from you.

If you have more than one cat or your cat shares your home with a dog, make sure to leave plenty of space between their feeding bowls. Cats who happily share their space with other pets can become territorial if they feel they have to watch over their shoulder while they eat. If you have a dog who likes to nibble on your cat's food, try to feed your kitty in a higher location.

Cats that live together can also be territorial when it comes to a favorite space. If one cat wants to sleep on the bed and finds the other cat already there, or if both want the same spot by a sunny window, or they both want to use the litter box at the same time, this can suddenly turn into a turf war, even if they both usually get along. Try to diffuse the situation by removing the cat that arrives second and finding an equally comfortable space for it and by making sure there is more than one litter box in your home. You can also use distraction if they are displaying the aggressive stare-down. Get out a toy they can both play with, such as a toy on a stick, and get them both involved in the game.

If there doesn't seem to be any rhyme or reason as to why your cat is suddenly territorial or aggressive, take it to your vet. Illnesses and injuries can often cause a feline to act out. So can loneliness and dirty litter boxes. Make sure to spend time with your cat and keep the box clean.

How fixing can fix aggression – and save lives at the same time

Intact cats, particularly males, tend to be more aggressive and territorial, and are more likely to bite or scratch which could injure you, a family member or another pet. A male cat's need to mate can also lead to dangerous cat fights and a driven desire to mark its territory with a pungent smelling spray. Male cats who are not neutered tend to roam great distances in search of a mate, leading to territorial disputes with other cats, nuisance behavior such as spraying and trespassing, and dangerous circumstances such as being hit by a car, catching an untreatable disease, or being picked up by animal control or taken to a shelter where it could be euthanized or adopted out.

Females who are not spayed can also be exhibit nuisance behavior in that they will be restless and may roam and howl to let males know they are ready to mate. Female cats are capable of getting pregnant by more than one male at a time and can produce several litters a year, thus contributing to the pet overpopulation epidemic that leads to the deaths of millions of unwanted pets each year.

"Fixing" your cat is a responsible way to resolve the many territorial and aggressive behaviors associated with a cat's desire and drive to reproduce. Both spaying and neutering are simple and safe procedures and there are many low cost and free spay and neuter clinics and programs for those who cannot afford the costs of sterilization. In addition, most shelters sterilize their cats prior to adopting them out, making the surgery part of the adoption fee. As an added bonus, cats that are spayed and neutered tend to live longer and healthier lives because sterilization can prevent breast, ovarian, uterine and testicular cancer, and reduce the risk of injury from territorial issues and of contracting incurable diseases. Plus, sterilization saves lives by preventing unwanted litters which opens up the opportunity to find homes for those cats that are already languishing at shelters nationwide.

Sitting on a Different Branch in the Evolutionary Tree

One misnomer about the evolution of housecats is that they are directly descended from big cats including tigers, lions, cheetahs, leopards and panthers. Another is that both domesticated cats and wild cats evolved from the sabertooth tiger. While it is true that our felines and those in the wild do share an earlier common prehistoric ancestor, a truer statement about their lineage is that the ancestral tree split into different branches, with wild cats and domestic cats each following their own evolutionary path.

This divergence in the tree resulted in the ancestors of our housecats seeking out and befriending humans, albeit originally for opportunistic reasons such as a never ending food source in the form of rodents who fed on human cultivated grains. Contrast this with the ancestors of today's big cats who never sought out human companionship and who today remain wild. One reason for this, researchers surmise, is that as domesticated cats evolved, they passed on a genome that affected temperament changes, whereas wild cats did not.

By comparing the genomes of wild cats to domesticated ones, researchers have found that housecats have more genetic mutations on genes that affect aggression, memory, and the ability to learn either from fear or from being rewarded. Early in the evolutionary game, as small cats became domesticated, these genes were passed on from one generation to the next, resulting in a cat that enjoys human company rather than its wild cousin who might fear humans or see us in terms of a meal.

Although it is undeniable that domesticated cats share many traits with wild cats, it is the ability and even desire to form bonds with us that separate the two related felines. Plus, living with a domesticated cat allows us to enjoy the best of its wild ancestors, without the threats associated with an animal that cannot be tamed. Cats straddle the fence, with two paws in the wild and two in the domestic world, but it is its preference to live in our company that makes it domesticated.

Perhaps the closest exception of this is the feral cat that exists on the fringes, either alone or in a feral community. Kittens learn to be social with humans from their mothers, but for feral kittens, this is often not the case, making it a poor pet and unlikely to ever be tamed. However, feral cat communities are complex and structured, and as long as these cats are fed by human volunteers and are part of a sterilization capture and release program, they do not need or desire to be anyone's pet. That doesn't mean their lives will be easy. Many feral cats face attacks from dogs, wild animals and even humans, and unless they are being fed by a volunteer group, they face the daily challenge of hunger and starvation, not to mention life threatening diseases.

Truly wild feral cats – as opposed to once-owned cats who have gotten lost or been abandoned and have learned to fend for themselves – rarely if ever are able to make the transition from wild to domestic pet. In this case, the feral cat more closely resembles its wild cousins. The difference, of course, is that given the chance at learning socialization prior to six-to-ten weeks of age, feral kittens can form bonds with humans, whereas wild cubs, even when raised in captivity, will retain their wildness.

Keeping Your Kitty Safe

No one can argue that cats are resilient creatures, which is probably where the nine lives myth stems from. But being blessed with an uncanny ability to survive does not mean that cats are indestructible. In fact, thousands of cats show up at veterinary hospitals each year with injuries, broken bones, poisonings and other serious ailments. Your duty as a cat owner is to make sure your home is safe and kitty-proof.

Keep Your Cat Indoors – No Matter What It Tells You

Don't listen to your cat when it tells you it would be happier if it was free to come and go. And don't listen to those people who believe that cats physically need this kind of freedom and that to make them indoor-only is actually cruel. The truth is, cats who are allowed to roam live shorter lives than indoor cats because of the many dangers lurking outside.

This can include irate neighbors who are tired of your cat roaming in their yards or upsetting their dogs. As shocking as it may be – not to mention against the law – people have been known to poison nuisance cats or take them to a nearby shelter and claim that a cat is a stray. Outdoor cats are also shot at with BB guns and arrows or tortured for sport or abused in some way.

Cats can also get trapped in other people's sheds or exposed to yard and other chemicals. Many an outside cat has died from licking antifreeze or from injuries sustained when finding warmth in a car engine during the winter and the car is started because the owner doesn't know the cat is there.

Outdoor cats run the risk of exposure to diseases that are spread airborne or from bites from other animals. Many of these diseases have no cures and can be life threatening. Outdoor cats can also pick up parasites and bring them home to you, your family and other pets.

If a cat is allowed outside, it also runs the risk of attacks from other cats, dogs or wild animals. Cats can also get lost or stolen, winding up in shelters or research laboratories. The number one way that outdoor cats die is from being hit by cars. Cats, like other animals, do not have a natural instinct that tells them to avoid oncoming traffic. If a cat is hit by a car, it may die instantly, but it also might endure a period of painful suffering prior to dying.

Cats who are allowed to roam can also be a threat to local birds and other small animals. Even if your cat is well fed, it may be hard to resist its natural instincts to hunt. Owned cats are responsible for killing hundreds of millions of birds each year.

Housecats need very little space to be happy, as evidenced by many city cats who are content in small apartments. What cats really need is a little of your time, and an environment that is mentally and physically stimulating. Indoor-only cats are often obese which can lead to chronic diseases. But due diligence on your part to make sure you exercise and mentally stimulate your cat through play, interactive toys and training, and not overfeeding it can make a world of difference in the happiness and health of your kitty.

If you do decide to allow your cat the freedom to come and go, at least make sure it is microchipped and up-to-date on its vaccinations. But keep in mind that cats who are allowed to roam live an average of two to four years, compared to 15-20 years for indoor cats. If you can, give your cat the best of both worlds by creating an enclosed outdoor space, such as a screened in patio or some type of enclosure that gives your cat the feeling of being in nature and the sun while staying safe. You also might try walking your cat on a leash or harness, although many felines do not enjoy being tethered. If none of these scenarios is possible, then make sure your cat has access to a sunny window where it can watch birds, squirrels, rabbits and outside activities that will keep it entertained.

Curiosity Can Kill Your Cat: Beware of Household Hazards

Just because you provide your cat with toys, doesn't mean you shouldn't supervise its play. Some toys can be choking hazards, as can string, yarn and ribbon. Never, ever let your cat chew on anything without you around. In addition to choking, many a cat has wound up in the vet emergency room due to obstructions in the intestines from these, as well as hair bands and other household items your cat might be attracted to.

Most cats hate baths and yet some are drawn to water. It is not unusual for a cat to drink out of faucets, jump in tubs, and be fascinated by a flushing toilet. However, make sure you always put the toilet seat down. Some cats like to drink out of toilets, but should yours fall in when you are not around it could drown, especially if it is still a kitten. If you treat your toilet water with any kind of cleaner, this can also prove fatal if your cat drinks it. Also, never leave water in a sink or tub. Your cat could drown if it falls in.

Cats can also be injured if they fall from high places. Provide a cat perch or cat tree for your kitty to satisfy its desire to be up high, and train it not to climb up on cabinets or book shelves. Also, shorten blind cords or wrap them up around the window latch, since a cat that gets tangled in a cord could die from asphyxiation.

Human medications are one of the most hazardous items for cats and a top reason for visits to veterinarian emergency rooms. Cats like the rattling sound of pill containers and often knock them off counters and then bat them around, only to eat any pills that fall out. Keep your prescriptions and over-the-counter medicines securely in your medicine cabinet. Also, be careful when you take medicine that you don't accidently drop any on the floor. In addition, be sure to follow the directions if you need to give your cat a medicine prescribed by your vet. Misuse in application is also common and can cause serious side effects. Never give your cat any pet medicines without your vet's knowledge and approval. And never, ever give your cat aspirin – a cat's body isn't able to process aspirin and this can lead to death.

Insecticides also pose a serious danger to cats. If you are having your home treated for insects or rodents, vacate the premises for a day or two. Ingesting an insecticide can cause serious health problems or death. Mice and rat poisons and baits can also threaten your cat's life if ingested. Also, be very careful when applying flea treatments to your cat. The misuse of flea and tick products, such as using a treatment made for dogs on a cat, is a widespread toxic occurrence.

Household cleaning products make many cats sick each year. Don't let your cat walk across a floor you've just mopped with floor cleaner or get in the shower if you've just cleaned it. Sometimes a cat will get the cleaning product on its paws and then get sick when it licks it off. Some products contain ingredients that taste good to cats, so put your cat in another room when you are using cleaning chemicals. If your cat is able to get inside the cabinets where you store cleaning products, install a baby latch.

Garden and fertilizer products can also be hazardous if your cat is allowed outside. Mulch can also be toxic, especially if it has been treated with chemicals. Antifreeze, paint thinner, drain cleaners, and pool and spa chemicals also pose a danger to cats.

Giving your cat people food can also put its health at risk. Grapes, raisins, avocados, food items containing xylitol, and chocolate can be especially toxic. Spicy foods can cause indigestion and stomach pain. And too much human food can lead to too many calories and weight gain.

Also, be aware of which plants you keep in your home. Azaleas, palm plants, rhododendron, lilies, ivy, schefflera, and poinsettias can all be toxic to cats. If you aren't sure about a plant, ask your vet or research it online. Even if a plant isn't toxic, some cats cannot resist a good nibble and may dig up the plant in the process, killing it and creating a mess. One way to satisfy your cat's desire to eat greenage is to purchase catnip and kitty grass you can grow inside.

Plastic bags can also pose a danger to cats, causing asphyxiation. Most cats can't resist getting inside a bag, but stash your plastic ones away. Also, remove and throw away dry cleaning bags, since your cat can easily become trapped inside them.

Cats are curious creatures – part of their charm and intelligence. But try to look for safety hazards around your home, much as you would do for a baby. Don't let your cat's curiosity be a reason it winds up harmed, injured, ill or worse.

The Dangerous Holidays

The holidays can be a fun and joyous time, so don't let yours be marred by an emergency visit to the vet. Your cat will pick up on the changes in your home as you decorate and move things around. It may not like these transformations, or it may be excited and curious about your decorations. Include your cat in the festivities, but take precautions for its safety as well.

Gift wrapping can be dangerous if your cat likes to chew on the ribbons. If your cat likes to do this, put presents with ribbons out of reach. Tinsel is also something many cats like to ingest, so consider decorating your tree without it. Also, be on the lookout for any decorations that have string-like parts that your cat might eat. Ribbons, strings and tinsel can cause intestinal blockages that may require an emergency vet visit and surgery.

Christmas trees are often a dangerous favorite to munch on for many cats. Discourage your cat from eating it by using a clicker and then a treat, since pine needles can make your cat sick and cause stomach and intestinal problems. Some cats like to drink the tree's water, which can contain chemicals to keep the tree fresh. Wrap a tree skirt around the bottom so that your cat isn't able to access the water. If all else fails, you might want to get an artificial tree.

Also, make sure any breakable ornaments are place out of your cat's reach, since these can break and cut your cat if they try to bat them around. Decorate the bottom of the tree with unbreakable plastic balls. Of course, there is always that cat who tries to climb the tree, knocking it down in the process. If this is your cat, keep the tree in a room where you can close the door when you aren't around to keep an eye on things.

You will need to be careful of holiday plants that are brought into your home. In addition to pine needles, some plants such as poinsettias, mistletoe and lilies can cause stomachaches and even death. If you aren't sure about a plant someone has given as a gift, keep it outside until you can contact your veterinarian.

Candles can also be a danger that you need to be vigilant about. Your cat probably could care less about the flame, but its tail could knock a candle over or get singed as it walks by. Considering burning tea lights instead, since these are placed safely in a container, out of reach of your cat's swishing tail.

Of course, the holidays mean foods and treats. Resist the urge to feed your cat leftovers, since these can have ingredients that are too rich for your cat causing stomachaches and diarrhea. Also,

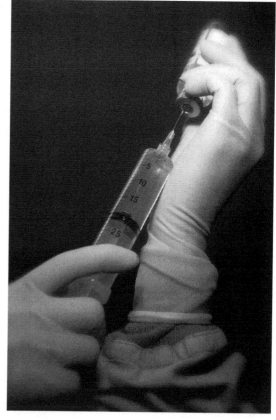

remember that chocolate can be fatal for cats, and turkey bones can splinter causing internal injuries. If you want your cat to be a part of the festive foods, buy it some cat treats.

If you are taking a road trip with your cat over the holidays, be sure to confine it in a cat carrier that is secured by a seatbelt. Make sure it is wearing its collar with identification, and that your cat is microchipped. If you are leaving your cat behind while you are gone, consider hiring a pet sitter to care for it in your home rather than boarding it at a kennel. Kennels are stressful places where cats can pick up illnesses and diseases, plus your cat won't understand where it is and may get depressed in thinking you have abandoned it. Your cat won't like you being away, but it will fare better being cared for in your home than in an unfamiliar place such as a kennel.

Finally, the holidays can be upsetting for your cat, with all the comings and goings of guests. If you have a party or company over, make sure your feline has a room it can retreat to. If you throw a holiday open house, keep your cat secure in a room and close the door. The last thing you need is your cat getting out and lost during this busy time of year.

The Dreaded But Necessary Vet Visit

Cats hate going to the vet. It's unfamiliar, and often involves getting checked out on a cold, steel table. It means being poked and prodded by a stranger, and then there's the waiting room filled with other cats and dogs.

Still, it is a necessary part of being a good cat owner. Check-ups can catch diseases and other ailments in their early stages, which can sometimes mean the difference between life and death. As a rule of thumb, your cat should get an annual check-up once a year – twice annually if your cat is over age ten. This way, your veterinarian can keep tabs on any changes from one year to the next, do blood work that might indicate any illnesses, and feel for any lumps. This is also a good time to have your cat vaccinated with any vaccines that might be due.

However, you should also take your cat to the vet *whenever* you spot any changes in your cat's behavior, personality, and demeanor. If your cat is an avid eater and then has lost interest in eating, this could indicate a serious illness. If your cat has suddenly lost weight, this might suggest cancer, diabetes or hyperthyroid disease. If your feline is limping or seems in pain, this could indicate an injury.

Eliminating outside the box or an increase in urination can also be indicative of illness, such as a urinary tract infection or diabetes. If your cat is normally active but now seems to have no energy, this might mean depression or a serious illness. The bottom line is, know your cat and report any changes you notice to your veterinarian.

The vaccine controversy

No doubt about it, vaccines can save lives. Being vaccinated against rabies, for example, can save your cat from being infected should it be bitten by a rabid animal, and prevent it from having to be quarantined by animal control if your cat were to bite or scratch someone. Feline panleukopenia, more commonly known as feline distemper, is also a core vaccine given to prevent this fast moving disease that can kill a cat in a matter of days.

There are also other recommended feline vaccines and their boosters, given either annually or every few years. Some prevent diseases while others lessen the severity should your cat contract them. These vaccines include rhinotracheitis, calicivirus, feline leukemia, chlamydophila, feline infectious peritonitis, bordetella, feline herpes virus, and feline immunodeficiency disease, and most veterinarians recommend your cat getting them.

But there is a growing concern among pet owners and even some veterinarians that we are over vaccinating our pets, leading to an increase in cancers, hyperthyroid disease, kidney damage, allergies and other ailments. For example, it has been suggested by some that the distemper vaccine can cause kidney damage later in life. Other pet owners claim that too many rabies vaccinations have caused paralysis and even death. And some cat owners report inflammation at the injection site that may lead to sarcoma cancer. Some research also suggests that while initial vaccines are fine, giving boosters is an overkill that can tax a pet's long term health. It is also recommended that you skip the combination shots, and have your cat given one vaccine at a time over several visits to avoid taxing your cat's immune system.

Often long term effects, such as cancer or skin allergies, don't show up until months or years later, and it is difficult to make the connection between the vaccine and the health repercussions. It has been suggested by some experts to ask your vet to do what is known as a *titer test*. This is a blood test that looks for anti bodies against certain diseases – if your cat has them then they do not need certain vaccine boosters or annual vaccinations because it has built up an immunity to the diseases. Some vets, however, don't believe that titer testing is reliable.

Many veterinarians agree that as your cat ages, you should limit its vaccines, especially if your cat is an indoor-only pet. Vaccinations can be especially taxing on the health of a senior cat. At what age should you stop vaccinating? This is difficult to determine, and something you should discuss with your vet, especially if your cat is over the age of 10.

There are laws in most areas that require that you vaccinate your cat against rabies, either on an annual basis or by getting a three-year vaccine. This can leave pet owners in a quandary in deciding whether to obey the law or limit their pet's vaccines. Also, many veterinarians will not treat pets that are not up-to-date on certain vaccines. It is therefore up to you to do your research about vaccines and their possible side effects so that you can make an informed choice about your cat's health. If your cat is an indoor-outdoor feline, then vaccines can be life saving. If your cat is indoors-only, then you will need to weigh the pros and cons or limit the types of vaccines your cat receives. Ultimately, it is your decision whether to vaccinate or not.

Chapter

13

When it is Time to Say Goodbye

I t may not be apparent at first, but your cat will slow down with age. You might notice that it hesitates before making a leap up on to its cat perch or your furniture, when it once did the jump without effort. Or your cat may walk more slowly, with more deliberate steps, just as an aging human does due to arthritic pain. Perhaps your cat doesn't appear to hear you when you call its name or doesn't seem to see something in close range or has lost its interest in play. Your kitty may seem to sleep more and eat less, or may lose its interest in treats it once found hard to resist.

These are all signs of aging, and one day it will happen to your cat. As your feline moves into its senior stage at about 10 years old, take it to your vet twice a year, and whenever something seems off about its general health in order to catch any ailments early. Cats are great at masking illness, so this will allow your vet to determine the progress of any potential health issues in order to give your cat the best chance of survival or at least the best quality of life. Some issues may simply be old age, such as arthritis, or losses of vision and sense of smell. This is also a time when teeth issues may emerge, so discuss the risks of dental cleaning versus not doing anything about it. If you decide not to go the dental cleaning route, which does involve anesthesia, then check out the many cat toothpaste products on the market and brush its teeth yourself.

Making Life Easier for Your Senior Cat

At this stage in your cat's life you want to make its day-to-day life as comfortable as possible. If your cat hesitates or avoids leaping on to the couch or bed, get it a step stool or pet stairs. Take time to brush your kitty daily, since many elderly cats start to neglect their grooming. Put an added pillow in its cat bed, so that its thinning body is cushioned and comfy. Also, make sure its cat bed is out of the way of drafts, since older cats can have a lower tolerance for cold.

If your cat seems to have a hard time getting into the litter box, it may be due to arthritic pain. Get a box with lower sides and be prepared for your cat to avoid covering its pee and poop. You also might want to provide several litter boxes throughout your home, so that your cat doesn't have to walk a long way in order to get to a box. In addition, you might want to feed it several small meals rather than two larger ones, since many senior felines experience intestinal issues.

Also, consider moving your cat's food and water near where it likes to hang out. A long trek to the kitchen may seem insurmountable to your cat now, so consider providing more than one food location. You may find that your cat drinks more water, which could indicate kidney failure. Or your cat may get dehydrated, so keep the water fresh and within easy reach, and consider switching to wet food only since this can add moisture to its diet. If either scenario occurs, consult with your veterinarian. Your cat's taste buds may be reduced, so it may not be as interested in eating. You might want to mix wet food with dry or add chicken broth to the food, to entice it to eat more.

If your cat seems irritated by another pet it has always considered a friend, make sure the other pet isn't trying to play aggressively or nose out your senior cat and claim its favorite spots. Also, think twice about getting a new cat at this time, especially a kitten. The stress may be too much for your elderly cat and a younger cat's energy levels may be more than it can bear.

Continue to try to play with your senior cat, because play stimulates both the body and mind. But customize the play sessions and keep them short, so that the interaction with you remains fun. Don't forget to include some catnip, which can be invigorating and tasty.

Your aging cat might also be grumpy, so be patient with its moodiness. Do what you can to make it comfortable, remove any obstacles, and repay its faithfulness with extra love and attention.

Being There When Your Cat Needs You Most

Like it or not, there will come a time when you will need to make end of life decisions for your cat. These will be difficult choices but it is good to plan it out before that day arrives. Cats can get sick at any age, but if you have an idea on how you'll handle it, it can make a painful time less confusing.

If you know your cat has a deadly disease, then ask your vet what signs you should look for in order to when it is time for you to have it euthanized. Sometimes cats that are suffering stop eating or they moan in pain, and some hide their distress. It is a little more difficult when something happens to your cat and you have to make a split second decision, such as if your cat is hit by a car and there is nothing your vet can do.

It would be easy if your cat just died naturally, in its sleep and without pain. But there is nothing natural about lingering in agony, and that is when you will need to intervene. Euthanizing your cat is an extremely difficult decision, maybe the hardest you will ever make, but it is also the kindest thing you can do for your cat when it is suffering and at the end of its life. Euthanasia provides a peaceful and painless way to allow a dying animal to pass away. It is actually a kind act, your last loving act, and one of the greatest final gifts you can give your cat.

If you must euthanize your cat, you may want to be at its side during the procedure. Some vet facilities don't allow this, but most today realize that owners emotionally need to have that final goodbye. Seeing your beloved cat being put to sleep may be too painful for you to witness. It is really a deeply personal choice and there is no right or wrong decision, but find out your options beforehand. If you decide you cannot handle seeing your cat put to sleep, then spend a few minutes saying goodbye. This can comfort your cat, and bring you peace in knowing that you were there when it needed you most.

A new kid on the block

After your cat has passed on, allow yourself as much time as you need to grieve. Surround yourself with family and friends who understand your loss. If you find yourself feeling depressed, consider attending a group for grieving pet owners. There are also many books on the subject of pet loss that can bring you comfort. It may be difficult to see your cat's old toys, feeding bowls and bed, so put these away if they cause you heartache. If you have had your cat's remains cremated, you might find comfort in creating a memorial in your yard, or have it buried in a pet cemetery so that you can visit its grave from time to time.

When you are ready, you might decide to adopt another cat. But don't rush the grief process or you might quickly regret the decision. You will know when it is the right time and when it is also the right cat. Don't be surprised if family and friends call about a cat that has just given birth to kittens that are now up for adoption. Choosing a cat is a deeply personal decision and they need to respect that and give you space.

Keep in mind that a new cat will never replace the one you've lost, nor will it have the same personality. That doesn't mean you won't find another feline who will also win your heart, but go by your gut feelings. You will know when a cat you meet is truly "the one."

Conclusion

I t will take time to learn your cat's language – but do take the time to learn it. By learning to speak cat, you will improve your life with your kitty and its life with you. Felines are complex and intelligent animals who enjoy our company. When you master cat communication, your cat in turn also learns to communicate with you.

As this book has demonstrated, cats communicate by sound, facial expressions, scent markings and body language. Picking up on these sometimes subtle nuances can improve your relationship with your kitty. Cats, in turn, quickly learn to understand both our verbal and physical commands. Use this book as a guide, but keep in mind that your cat will have some ways of talking to you that is unique to it alone.

Always remember that when your cat acts out and behaves inappropriately, such as eliminating outside the litter box or scratching up the back of the couch, it is not trying to be bad or annoy you, but rather it is its attempt to let you know that something is wrong. Never punish your cat; instead try to see your home environment from its perspective.

Also, take time to enjoy the marvel of two different species living under the same roof with the potential ability to communicate with each other even though you each speak a different language. This joyful mystery includes your cat's capacity to love you and be affectionate, and in turn willingly accept your love and affection. Never take for granted the evolutionary wonder of this special relationship between humans and cats. Learning to speak feline is an important and necessary part of this process that can make your lives together meaningful and special.

Glossary

Allogrooming: A group form of grooming where cats lick and clean each other as a form of affection and to cement the bonds of their relationships.

Breed true: Selective breeding over several generations that results in the ability to consistently produce offspring that are the same as the parents with set traits in looks, size, color, hair length and personality.

Bunchers: People who capture strays or steal owned cats and sell them to research laboratories.

Cardiomyopathy: A common heart condition found in cats that affects a cat's left heart ventricle, in which the heart chamber becomes thickened, scarred or dilated. Left untreated, it will lead to death.

Carnivore: An animal that consumes meat.

Crepuscular: An animal that hunts at dawn and dusk.

Cheyletiella: Mites that live on a cat's skin, causing an itchy rash and skin irritations.

Clowder: A group of cats.

Cuterebra: Parasites complete their life cycle under a cat's skin, sometimes leading to secondary illnesses.

Cystitis: Also known as *Feline Lower Urinary Tract Disease (FLUTD)*, it is an inflammation or infection of a cat's bladder that can be acute or chronic, and is caused by a bacterial infection or by urinary stones or crystals.

Declaw: To remove the nail and often the first joint on a cat's front paws.

Diurnal: An animal that is active during both the day and night.

Domestication: To tame an animal, by generations of breeding, to live in close association with humans, so that the animal loses its ability to live in the wild.

Euthanasia: The act of painlessly putting an animal to death; often called *putting to sleep*.

Familiar: During the Middle Ages, it was a term used for a witch that took the form of an animal, usually a cat.

Feline Immunodeficiency Virus Infection: Also known as *Feline Aids* or *FIV*, is a retrovirus that suppresses a cat's immune system, leading to secondary diseases.

Feline Infectious Peritonitis Virus: Also known as *FIP*, it is often fatal and can affect a cat's white blood cells causing intense inflammatory reactions around vessels in the abdomen, kidneys or brain.

Feline Leukemia: Also known as *FeLV*, it is a highly contagious virus shed in saliva, nasal secretions, urine, feces and an infected mother cat's milk. FeLV can cause cancer, blood disorders and a lowered immune system, making a cat susceptible to other diseases.

Feline Panleukopenia: Also known as *Feline Distemper* or

FPV, it is a highly contagious, life threatening disease that affects rapidly dividing bloods cells, leading to anemia and a susceptibility to contracting other diseases.

Felis sylvestris: A wildcat originating in the Middle East 12,000 years ago that is believed to be the ancestor of today's housecat.

Feral: A cat born outside from a feral mother or that is abandoned outside by its mother prior to weaning that never learns socialization skills. Not to be confused with homeless cats that once had human-cat relations but now fend for themselves outside.

Fix: Also known as *fixing*, is to sterilize a cat making it unable to reproduce. Female cats are *spayed*, whereas male cats are *neutered*.

Giardia: Parasites that live in a cat's intestinal tract, causing diarrhea.

Head bunting: Also known as *head butting* or *head bumping*, where a cat leans in and butts a person's head as a display of affection or friendliness.

Herbivore: An animal that consumes plants.

Hyperthyroidism: Also known as *Hyperthyroid Disease*, it attacks a cat's thyroid, causing an excessive concentration of the thyroidal hormone thyroxine, causing dramatic weight loss, excessive thirst, increased urination, and an unquenchable appetite. Untreated, it can cause death.

Kneading: A form of physical communication where a cat alternatively presses with one front paw and then the other as if it is kneading dough. Used by kittens to express the milk out of their mother's teats, and later by adult cats on their owners as a form of affection and happiness.

Megacolon: A condition where a cat's large intestine and colon become enlarged and filled with hard fecal matter, making it unable to contract effectively in order to evacuate the stool.

Microchip: An animal implant the size of a grain of rice that is part of a network and contains information used to identify the owner in the event that the animal is lost or stolen.

Moggie: A mixed breed cat.

Neuter: The surgical procedure of sterilizing a male cat so that it is unable to reproduce.

Nictitating membrane: Also known as a cat's *third eyelid*, it is a protective pale pink membrane that comes out from the inner corner of a cat's eye, partially covering the cat's eye when it is ill or its eye has been injured.

Nocturnal: Active at night.

Obligate carnivore: An animal who must consume meat as part of its diet, or its health will deteriorate.

Obstipation: The inability of a cat to empty its colon due to chronic constipation.

Omnivore: An animal that consumes both plants and meat.

Proprioceptor: A sensory organ located on the tips of the whiskers that sends signals to a cat's brain and nervous system which helps a cat be aware of its surroundings, particularly in the dark, and be able to gauge the size and width of spaces.

Pseudaelurus: A prehistoric cat-like animal originating in Central Asia, believed to be the original ancestor of wild and domestic cats.

Purebred: An animal who is descended over several generations from one particular lineage or breed. Also known as a *pedigree*.

Renal failure: Kidney failure that can be *acute* or *chronic*.

Spay: The surgical procedure of sterilizing a female cat so that it is unable to reproduce.

Titer test: A blood test that looks for anti bodies against certain diseases a cat has previously been vaccinated against.

Upper Respiratory Infection: Also known as *URI*, is a variety of contagious infections derived from viruses or bacteria that can affect a cat's nose, throat and sinus area.

Urinary Tract Infection: Also known as *UTI*, it is an infection in the bladder caused by bacteria, bladder stones, fungus, parasites, urinary stones, viruses or cancer, making it difficult and painful for a cat to urinate.

Uroliths: Also known as *Urinary Tract Stones* that form in a cat's bladder and can cause painful urination that can eventually lead to death.

Vibrissae: The stiff, strong and hard hair, also known as *whiskers*, on a cat's face, back of the front legs and head that work as receptors.

Author Biography

K.O. Morgan is the author of *The Complete Guide Interpreting Your Own Dreams and What They Mean to You*, *The Complete Guide to Pruning Trees and Bushes: Everything You Need to Know Explained Simply*, and the Kindle e-book, *Living Smart: Healing Foods*. She is also a writer of magazine articles, blogs and mini books. She has been published in *Produce Business*, *Deli Business*, *American Food & Ag Exporter*, and *Living in Hampton Roads* magazines; and has written three published mini books entitled *Living Smart: Healing Foods*, *Living Smart: Boosting Brain Power*, and *1001 Internet Freebies*. K.O. Morgan resides with her husband, daughter and three cats in historic Hampton Roads, Virginia. Find her online at **http://www.kimomorgan.com**.

Index

-A-

Aggression: 97, 127, 134, 201, 202, 243, 250, 251, 253, 255, 9, 10
Aging: 269, 272, 127, 199
Allogrooming: 128, 148, 277
Alpha: 239
Arthritic: 269, 271

-B-

Boredom: 58, 142, 155, 203, 216, 240

-C-

Cancer: 48, 51, 107, 163, 165, 172-174, 182, 183, 185, 186, 254, 266, 267, 278, 281, 8
Carnivores: 43, 45

Cat kissing: 68, 122
Cat Sign Language: 143, 7
Chatter: 92, 114
Clowder: 239, 277, 9
Constipation: 161-164, 280, 7
Crepuscular: 73, 74, 212, 277
Cystitis: 166, 167, 278, 7

-D-

Declaw: 39, 40, 168, 278
Declawing surgery: 39
Discipline: 135, 191, 198, 200, 9

-E-

Euthanize: 272

-F-

Feline aids: 107, 178, 278, 8
Feline communication: 111

Feline distemper: 180, 266, 278, 8

Feline leukemia: 107, 174, 266, 278, 8

Felis sylvestris: 18, 21, 279

-H-

Head bunting: 120, 121, 279

Heart disease: 174, 175, 8

High Rise Syndrome: 62

Household hazards: 260, 10

Hyperthyroid disease: 75, 129, 162, 171, 175, 183, 184, 266, 279, 8

-K-

Kitty presents: 130, 7

Knead: 68, 117, 118, 221, 248, 7

-L-

Lethargy: 162, 182, 8

Liger: 26

-M-

Moggie: 87, 89, 280, 6

-N-

Neutered: 31, 32, 46, 49, 119, 120, 253, 254, 279, 5

-P-

Pedigree: 90, 92, 102, 280

Pregnancy: 48, 51

Pseudaelurus: 20, 280

-S-

Spayed: 31, 32, 46, 48, 49, 119, 120, 253, 254, 279, 5

Special needs: 81, 103-106, 109, 6, 96

Sterilization: 31, 47-49, 254, 255

Superstitions: 69, 6

-T-

Territorial: 22, 48, 93, 237, 240, 242, 243, 251-254, 10

Tigon: 26

Tone: 100, 134-136, 138, 200, 13, 14, 17, 126, 99

Toxoplasmosis: 51, 52

Training: 50, 136, 139, 140, 142, 153, 155, 189, 191, 195, 198, 213, 259, 11, 14, 21, 138, 188, 212, 9

Tummy rollover: 116, 7

-U-

Upper respiratory infection: 177, 178, 281, 8

Urinary tract infection: 163, 183, 198, 266, 281, 7

Urinary tract stones: 167, 281, 7